Handbook of
Sales Humor for
All Situations

Handbook of
Sales Humor for
All Situations

Henri Saint-Laurent

PARKER PUBLISHING COMPANY, INC. *West Nyack, N.Y.*

© 1971 by

PARKER PUBLISHING COMPANY, INC.

West Nyack, N.Y.

Library of Congress
Catalog Card Number: 77-156765

Printed in the United States of America
ISBN 0-13-380840-8
B & P

Dedication

To my wife, Betty, who has listened to me for forty years and I have the jokes to prove it.

To my three sons (there is a title for a T.V. show) Bruce, Chuck and Jay who have listened to my humor with splendid expressions of indifference.

How to Use
Humor in Selling

A sense of humor in selling, when used appropriately and discreetly, is an effective sales tool in the hands of a salesman who definitely "handles it with care." Moreover, using humor will make selling more fun—fun with a purpose—and add zest to your life at home and at play.

Here is a list of selling situations when humor can often be used to sell more, easier and faster.

- As an "ice-breaker" for cold calls, instead of giving a weather report.
- As a "warm-up" for repeat calls. (The one-liners and definitions in Part II and Part III of this book are ideal as "openers.")
- As a change-of-pace for lengthy presentations.
- As "seasoning" for "flat" sales talks.
- To maintain interest in you and your presentation.
- To favorably "condition" the sales interview.
- To accent selling points, sales features or customer benefits.
- To ease an uncomfortable selling atmosphere.
- To "bail out" of an awkward selling situation.
- To remove tensions, relieve pressures and relax your customers.
- To put your customer in a buying mood.
- To wrap-up and clinch the "wavering sale."
- To earn you a welcome on your next call.
- To help you express your ideas more interestingly and effectively to buying committees or groups of prospects.

7

Let's talk about old jokes before discussing the selection and delivery of funny stories. An old joke that still sounds funny is much more humorous than a new original funny story that does not tickle the "funny-bone." Any joke which is still around after years, decades, must have a basic appeal, and this basic appeal could be lost trying to find something "new" just for the sake of something "new."

Let's not forget, the humor you may consider old, more often than not, will be new to your listeners, and any stories your customers haven't heard are new to them. Remember, "There are no old jokes, just old listeners." It has been said that a humorous speaker is a guy with a good memory, who hopes no one else has one.

Here are a dozen suggestions on selecting and telling all types of jokes.

1. Don't use any humor unless you really enjoy hearing a funny story. You should genuinely enjoy telling a funny story and find that what you think is funny, others do, too. You can readily remember funny stories and you can tell them well enough to get laughs.

2. Don't ever use humor in selling when it isn't appropriate to the mood of the sales interview and to the character of the buyer.

3. Rely on your first favorable impression of the funny story that you have heard or read; it probably will be the one you should repeat and use because it will fit your style and personal image. However, if a question comes up in your mind about whether to use a particular story or not, then the answer is: "Don't" This also holds true of the use of four-letter words. "Don't."

4. Be sure to be "sold" on the joke you select, and that it also fits the selling situation, before using it. Yet, don't enjoy your humor so much that you laugh louder than your listeners. Nor should you tend to use humor so much that your customers prefer your stories better than what you are selling.

5. Before telling your funny story publicly, give it a "trial-run" at home—to your family and friends. As their reactions dictate, use it again, revise it, or forget it.

Practice telling the story with light precision, fluency and use only enough wordage to insure a clear meaning of the punch line. Build up the punch line and not the story.

6. Don't clumsily "drag in" a joke for the sole purpose of being humorous, unless your funny lines can stand up by themselves as appropriate and related to the selling point you are making. If your gag is an apt "for instance," yet "bombs," you still have illustrated and underscored your point in an interesting and effective manner. Note, don't try to neutralize the "bomb," go on to your next point.

7. Personalize or slant your jokes to well-known people; this will magnify the effect. However, don't ever downgrade or embarrass anyone; if someone is to be the "goat" make sure it's yourself.

8. Localize your humor to give it "home-style" flavor, befitting the background of your listeners or the products or services you are selling.

9. Always glide into your humor casually and without announcing your attempt to be funny. In the same casual manner, slip back into the context of your sales presentation, but without saying so specifically. For example, don't say, "Here's a funny," then afterward say, "Now to be serious again."

10. To get maximum surprise and dramatic impact, disguise the "punch-line," until you come into the "home-stretch," then belt it, loud and clear, while maintaining face-to-face contact with your listeners.

11. It is important not to forget to pause after telling your funny, so that you give your listeners time to laugh, but don't step on your laughs.

12. When telling "He said" and "She said" types of stories, indicate the change from one to the other, by talking from one side then the other side. Also, make a change in your tone of voice as you change the characters. Speaking of tones, don't degrade anyone by telling stories in dialect, particularly a dialect with an accent.

HOW TO USE THIS HANDBOOK OF HUMOR

Read one Alphabetical Section or Part at a time. When you come across something you like, and it fits your style and image, put a pencil check-mark alongside it. Later, review the humor you have checked off, and if it still hits your funny-bone, write it down on a 3 x 5 card. Memorize it, revise it, and give it a "trial-run." If it passes the test, then adapt it to your sales presentations and have profitable fun in selling.

Henri Saint-Laurent

ACKNOWLEDGMENT

It has been said that a joke usually doesn't belong to the one who told it last, rather, it belongs to the one who is telling it now, and it only belongs to him until someone else re-tells the joke.

However, I want to acknowledge with thanks the countless hundreds of salesmen, sales executives and sales speakers who have shared their favorite "funnies" with me, and special thanks to:

Peter W. Bove
Joseph J. Curtin
Zenn Kaufman
John H. Marsh
Paul J. Micali
Frank C. Pesveyc
John H. Wolfe
Joseph L. Wood
Dave Yoho

CONTENTS

Handbook of
Sales Humor for
All Situations

Part I
JOKES FOR SALESMEN

A

ACTIVATE THE PINS

The president and sales manager were looking gloomily at a map of their territory, with pins showing the locations of salesmen.

"Frankly," said the sales manager to the president, "I think we have only one choice. Let's take the pins out of the map and stick 'em in the salesmen!"

ACTIVE WIDOW

Census taker: "When did your husband die?"
Widow: "Six years ago."
Census taker: "But you told me that you have a son four years old and one girl who is two years old. How come?"
Widow: "It was my husband who died, not me!"

AFTER-DINNER SPEECH

One after-dinner speech that brings regret and sorrow is the one where the man of the house says, "I'm too tired now. I'll do the dishes tomorrow!"

AGELESS BUCK-PASSING

We're now in an era where one generation pays the last generation's debts by issuing bonds for the next generation to pay!

AGING HAT

The officer pulled the motorist to the side of the road and

exclaimed, "When I saw you come zooming around that curve I said to myself '45' at least!"

"Well, you're wrong officer," protested the woman driver. "This hat just makes me look older."

ALL ALONE

The food salesman said, "I hate to see a woman dine alone."
The liquor salesman said, "I hate to see a woman drink alone."
The mattress salesman only smiled.

ANNIVERSARY BREATH

The sales manager asked the salesman, "Is that the smell of booze on your breath?"

"Yes," replied the salesman, "I've been celebrating the tenth anniversary of the raise you gave me."

ANNIVERSARY KISSES

The stingy salesman, while on an out-of-town sales trip, sent his wife a check for a million kisses as an anniversary present.

The wife was quite annoyed and sent back a post-card: "Dear Chuck, thanks for the anniversary check. The milkman cashed it for me just this morning!"

APPRAISAL SYSTEM

The man wondered why it was that his friend had so much luck with the used cars he bought; he never seemed to have any trouble with them. So one day he asked his friend how he managed to choose so wisely.

"I don't understand it," the man said. "After all, you know very little about cars."

"That's true," admitted the other, "but I've got a system. You see, I get a car on approval and then right away drive to another used car dealer and tell him I want to sell it. In the next few minutes he's told me everything that's wrong with it."

APPROPRIATELY SIZED

You can tell who handles the money in the family these days. They're making women's purses bigger and men's wallets smaller.

ARMED BANKER

It used to be that a man needed a college degree and a course in accounting to go into the banking business. Now all he needs is a gun.

AT HOME IN THE AIR

The airlines are now using married women as stewardesses. I don't mind that, but why do they have to serve morning coffee in an old robe, have their hair in curlers and wear dirty old sneakers?

ATTACK INSURANCE

There are so many muggings, that when secretaries work late, they won't go home alone by themselves anymore. They wait for their managers to take them home. At least, then if they get attacked, it could mean a raise!

"AT-TENTION, PRIVATES!"

Two political candidates were debating.

"Vote for me," said the first, "I was a general, a man of great responsibility. My opponent was not."

"It's true," said the second, "he was a general and I a private. All of you who were generals vote for him—privates, vote for me!"

AUTOMATED NOODLES

"Did you hear that XYZ Macaroni automated five years ago? That was using their noodles!"

AUTOMATIC WARNING

A salesman on a recent flight noticed that one of the stewardesses coming out of the pilot's cabin appeared quite flustered. She went back to the other stewardess and told her something in a low voice, yet loud enough for the eavesdropping salesman to hear: "Watch yourself if you go up forward. They've got the automatic pilot on!"

B

BACHELOR'S NAG

The executive, who had separated from his wife, was asked how he was getting along, living alone.

He smugly replied, "Great. Once a week I have a woman come in and nag."

BACK-TO-BACK STYLING

There's a new version, this year, of the fastback auto. The Volkswagen Company has a model called the square-back and the way the trend is going in auto styling, the next one will probably be called the hunchback.

BACKYARD CONSULTANT

A woman asked a new acquaintance, "What does your husband do?"

Her new friend told her, "He's a consultant."

"What is a consultant?" the first lady asked.

The second lady replied, "I think I can best explain what a consultant is by telling you an experience we had with our tom cat."

"Our male cat," she continued, "was so dedicated to feline nocturnal activities, that the neighbor who owned cats of the opposite sex complained. As the result, we took our over-sexed tom to the vet and had him fixed. He still goes out every night, but now he's only a consultant."

BALANCED ADVICE

The businessman was emphatically told that if he wanted to survive, he had to give up wine, women and song—not by his doctor, by his accountant.

BALANCING THE BALANCE

Mrs. Wheeler, a newlywed, received a call from her bank.

"I want to inform you," said the business-like voice on the phone, "that as of the first of August, your checking account is overdrawn to the amount of $102.10."

"Is that so?" said Mrs. Wheeler, who paused for a few seconds to determine what her husband, Henry, would say in such a situation. Finally she said, "Will you do me a favor? Will you look up my balance for the first day of July?"

"Certainly," said the bank clerk and them came back to report, "On the 1st of July, you had a balance of $320.02."

"See," said Mrs. Wheeler, "and did I call you up? However, I'm sending you a check for $102.10. That should balance my account."

BALL HANDLING

Secretary: "I went bowling last night and found out that my bowling is much better than my golf!"

Boss: "How come?"

Secretary: "Well, I bowled all night and didn't lose a single ball!"

BANG-UP JOB

An auto salesman sold a man a second car—a tow truck.

The man explained, "Every time my wife parks the car, she does a bang-up job and merely says, 'well, that's the way the Mercedes-Benz!' "

BANK MERGER

It was love at first sight at the bank. She was in the withdrawal line and he was at the deposit window.

BARE REASON

First wife: "What color dress are you wearing to the sales award dinner?"

Second wife: "We're supposed to wear something to match the color of our husband's hair. What will you wear?"

First wife: "Gracious me! I don't think I'll go."

BARTENDER'S CHOICE

A man rushes up to the bar, orders a double shot of Canadian Club, gulps it down, leaves a $5 bill on the bar, and walks out.

Bartender, after pocketing the $5 bill: "How about that? This guy leaves a $5 tip and doesn't pay for the drink!"

BARTENDER'S TRIM

The drunk collapsed on the bar, his head down.

"Gimme a drink," he mumbled.

The bartender replied, "Not in here. Look at you, you can't even raise your head."

The drunk answered, "Okay, gimme a hair-cut!"

BAWLING START

The nurse was asked by a hospital visitor why all the babies in the nursery were bawling.

She retorted, "Listen, if you were only a few days old, without any clothes and owed almost $2300 on the national debt, you'd be bawling too!"

BE YOUR OWN CUSTOMER

A woman commented to a spinster-type sales girl at the perfume counter:

"Well if it does àll that to men, why are you still here?"

BEACH PLAYTHINGS

"Don't lie to me," the irate woman screamed to her executive husband. "Helen saw you at the convention, playing around on the beach in Miami with a blonde!"

"Well, what d'you expect at my age," was the retort, "a pail and shovel?"

BEAUTIFUL CHOICE

Three salesmen were discussing what they considered the most beautiful thing in the world.

Gene said, "I say a beautiful woman is the most beautiful thing in the world."

Ed claimed, "Sleep is the most beautiful thing in the world."

Tom agreed, saying, "Ah yes, next to a beautiful woman, sleep is!"

BEDROOM TROUBLES

A sales executive called on his physician. "I'm an absolute wreck," he complained. "I'm nervous, tense and I can't sleep."

"That's because you insist upon taking your troubles to bed with you," the physician pointed out.

"Who can avoid it?" the patient asked. "My wife refuses to sleep alone."

BEFORE AND AFTER MOOD

A Salesman asked the receptionist when the best time was to see the purchasing agent.

She replied, "Take your choice. Before lunch, his mind is irritable and after lunch, his stomach is irritable."

BELATED CONFIDENCE

The town scrooge was asked how he got started in the banking business and he explained, "One day I put up a sign that read

'Bank' in one of my unrented stores. A local man came in and gave a $100 and another gave me $200 and another $500. Well, by that time my confidence reached such a point, that I put in $75 of my own money."

BENEFITS WENT BANKRUPT

The sales job hunter, who was discussing his previous job with a potential employer said, "In my last job, I had a big life-insurance policy, a month's vacation with pay and a $1000 holiday bonus."

The potential boss asked, "Then why did you leave?"

The applicant replied, "The company went bankrupt."

BETTER OR WORSE

Business was a bit dull in town, so the carpet-sweeper salesman thought he'd try a rural district.

When he began his sales talk, the hillbilly interrupted with, "Don't waste your breath. I got a carpet sweeper."

The salesman, alert for the opening, said, "Good. I can make you a generous allowance on your old sweeper in part payment on this splendid new model."

The hillbilly seemed tempted, then shook his head. "No," he said, "I can't make that kind of a deal. After all, I took her for better or wuss."

BIG CANCELLATION

A salesman was boasting to another salesman, "I just got an order for $50,000."

"I don't believe it," answered the other salesman.

"You don't believe it? Here, I'll show you the cancellation!"

BIGGEST LOVER

On a jet flight to New York, a 300-pound executive was quietly reading his paper when a stewardess asked if he would care for a cocktail. Not looking up he replied, "I'm a lover, not a drinker."

The stewardess' reaction was a surprised, "Oh?"

"In fact," he continued, putting his paper down and giving her his full attention, "I'm probably the third greatest lover in history."

"Is that right?" said the stewardess. "And who would you say No. 1 and No. 2 were?"

"John Adams and Grover Cleveland," declared the 300-pounder.

"But they weren't great lovers," protested the stewardess.

"Oh, my gosh," he said slapping his gigantic thigh, "then I must be No. 1!"

BIRTH CONTROL LEASE

A real estate agent rented an apartment for a client who insisted on no children.

The real estate agent found a childless couple and had them sign a lease which read, $200 a month for light, water, heat, and the pill.

BLACKED-OUT VIEWING

Selling used television sets, the salesman commented, "This one is as good as new. It belonged to an old lady who didn't like talk shows, game shows, westerns, Marcus Welby, Mod Squad and Dean Martin."

BLIND HIT

Two cars banged into each other. "What's the matter with ya? Are you blind?" the first driver yelled.

The other promptly countered, "Blind? I hit ya, didn't I?"

BLOODY DIAGNOSE

The town drunk staggered into the doctor's office and complained that he wasn't feeling his old self. "Tell me, Doc," he pleaded, "what's wrong with me?"

After a brief examination, the doctor explained, "George, it seems you're letting a little too much blood get into your alcohol system!"

BOARD CHAIRMAN'S EQUAL

A sales training manager was almost at his wits end. A trainee continually started long-winded discussions on trivial matters, asked pointless questions, and in general disrupted the entire training program. Finally the trainer told him, "You know, you have a great deal in common with the chairman of the board of this company."

"I have?" said the trainee, pleased. "How do you mean?"

Replied the trainer, "You're both as high in this company as you'll ever get!"

BOOMERANGED SALES POINTER

Part of the sales manager's training session included the point that when making a sales presentation the salesman should repeat, repeat, repeat the specific benefits of the product, because constant repetition in a sales talk has an emotional impact toward getting a favorable decision.

One salesman spoke up, "O.K., now I'd like to try that technique on you. Can I get a raise, a raise, a raise?"

BORING EXPERT

A highly touted "expert" on salesmanship was addressing a meeting of more than 500 salesmen. After he had droned on for more than an hour, his audience became obviously restless, chairs were scraping and a number of men were leaving the room. Finally the exasperated speaker said, "There's so much commotion out there I can hardly hear myself speaking."

"Forget it," shouted a bored salesman. "You're not missing a thing!"

BOTTLED BENEFITS

A door-to-door salesman said to a modern homemaker, answering the door chimes, "I'm selling something that will make you popular, happier and make you many new friends, too!"

"Great, I'll take a fifth!"

BRAGGART'S DILEMMA

One salesman's wife had no alternative, she couldn't brag that her husband's salary was raised from $12,000 to $16,000 because she had already bragged that he was making $20,000.

BRAINS FOR SALE

An advertising salesman boarded a train and took a roomette. He carried only a small bag, and the porter inquired about his other luggage.

"I haven't any," said the advertising man.

"But you're a salesman, ain't you?" asked the porter.

"That's right, I am, but I don't need a lot of luggage. I sell brains."

"Huh!" said the porter. "You're the first salesman that ever rode this train without samples."

BREAKDOWN SELLING PLAN

The salesman insisted on buying the worst heap in the used car lot.

Car salesman: "Why this piece of junk?"

Salesman: "This looks like the car that most likely will break down."

Car salesman: "Why in the world do you want a car that will surely break down?"

Salesman: "When this car breaks down, a crowd will gather around me and then I'll sell them my line of brushes."

BREATH OF A SALESMAN

Recently, a vice-president in charge of marketing sent to all salesmen the following directive:

"Effective immediately, you are to desist having vodka-based cocktails with customers. If you must drink, order drinks that leave a breath that tells. Therefore, your customer guest will realize that you are drunk, not stupid."

BROAD EXPLANATION

The salesman had finally agreed to take his wife on his next selling trip. Entering the hotel elevator at the first stop, a sexy-looking blonde, waiting in the elevator, looked at them in surprise and said, "Hi John, how are you?"

When the salesman and his wife reached their room, she demanded, "Who was that broad?"

"Don't make matters worse, Helen," replied the husband, "I'm going to have plenty of trouble explaining *you* to *her!*"

BUG COOLER

A Texan asked if his VW was air-conditioned.

"No," he said, "but I always keep a couple of VWs in the deep freeze!"

BURNING FACT

Newly insured merchant: "What would I get if my store should burn tonight?"

Insurance salesman: "Probably about ten years!"

BUSINESS AFLOAT

Two business partners were fishing in a small rowboat, and suddenly a storm came up. The boat capsized, and while one of the men began to swim, his partner floundered and sputtered helplessly. He was sinking.

"Say, Fred," the swimmer said to the sinking man, "can you float alone?"

"Look!" screamed the other, "I'm drowning, and you talk business!"

BUSINESS CARD BARGAIN

The office secretary presented the salesman's card to her boss, who promptly tore it in two and tossed it in the trash basket. "Tell him I can't see him," the boss snorted.

But when the secretary delivered the message, the salesman smiled, "Then ask him if I may have my card back; they're expensive."

Sputtering, the boss gave his secretary a quarter for the salesman. When the girl delivered the coin, the salesman gave her another card, "Tell him they're two for a quarter," he said.

The salesman got to see his client.

BUSINESS HAS GONE TO—

A preacher admonishing his flock on evils of business wound up his sermon with, "And remember my friends, there will be no buying and selling in Heaven."

A man in back row grumbled, "That's not where business has gone anyway."

BUSINESS REPORT

Freight car loadings were down 27% last week. The consumption of alcoholic beverages was up 32%. This proves that more people are getting loaded than frieght cars!

BUYING IN REVERSE

A woman brought into the antique shop an old end table and asked the shop owner how much he would give for it.

Yankee Trader: "$7.00"

Antique shopper: "Certainly it's worth more!"

Yankee Trader: "Of course not. Look at the cracks and how the legs are loose!"

Antique shopper: "Okay, I saw this end table in front of your shop with a $25 price tag and I brought it in and now I'll take it, for $7.00."

C

CAGEY HUSBAND

A salesman's wife had been bugging him for a mink for months. He finally gave in and promised her one for her birthday, but on one condition—she has to keep it's cage clean.

CALENDARED QUESTION

After a long-winded talk the sales expert asked, "Are there any questions?"

A salesman spoke up, "What day is it?"

CALCULATING DEVICES

The average sales office has numerous calculating devices. Some are machines, some are secretaries.

CALL THE BULL PEN

It was at a meeting of the sales executives club of a New England city about a week before their annual award dinner, when a committee was named to approach a leading industrialist, informing him that he was expected to be at the award dinner the following week.

The committee duly approached the man, and the chairman said, "The reason we'd like to have you at the dinner is because we're going to name you 'Man of the Year.' "

"It's a great honor," was the industrialist's reply, "but I have to be in New York for an important business meeting. I'm sorry, but I just won't be able to attend."

"No sweat," replied the committe chairman. "I guess we'll have to find somebody else."

CALL TO DUTY

An Office manager asked the clerks gathered around the coffee machine, "Anybody interested in a little overtime to get some work out?"

CALLS OR STOPS

The sales manager had been admonishing his salesmen to make more calls. One morning a salesman excitedly reported, "Boss! I made 39 calls yesterday. I would have made more, but some character asked me what I was selling!"

CANDID CAMERA

One bank president doesn't like the new bank cameras. It caught a few bandits, to be sure. But it also got some beautiful shots of him and his secretary.

CANINE'S OBJECTION

If he sold a certain suit in stock, the apprentice salesman was told he could have a steady job as a clothing salesman. The suit in question was a beaut—light purple with thin white stripes and yellow dots.

An hour later, clothes in disarray and bloody, he rushed to the manager and shouted, "I sold it!"

"Looks as if you had a lot of customer resistance," said the boss.

"No, I didn't have any trouble with the customer," the young man explained, "but what a fight I had with his seeing-eye dog!"

CAPITALISTIC EXPLANATION

During a Russian visitor's tour of an automobile factory, he stopped to chat with a worker. "Why," he asked, "do you prefer the capitalistic system to the communistic system?"

"Let me explain," said the worker, drawing a deep breath. "Say it's about quitting time and you're standing on the corner waiting for a bus and a big black limousine comes along. It stops in front of you, and you see it's your boss. He tells you to hop in and you drive away. He says, 'How about coming to my estate for a swim?' so you go, and when you finish he serves you a tall cool drink, and invites you to stay for dinner, and a few more tall cool drinks, and the boss suggests you stay overnight. You do, and after a delicious breakfast, you drive back to the factory with the boss. That is why I like capitalism."

"Good heavens," gasped the astonished Russian, "Has that happened to you?"

"No," admitted the worker, "but it's happened to my sister twice."

CAPTIVE AUDIENCE

A television rating outfit phoned a thousand men to ask, "Who are you listening to right now?"

83% replied: "My wife!"

CASH FRIEND

A salesman opening a new territory in Texas called on his first dealer to find him unusually friendly and constantly calling him "Podner."

Warming to his sales message, the salesman handed the Texan a 50-cent cigar.

"Why, thank you, podner," he said, "I shore enjoy a good cigar!"

Finally, after securing a fair-sized order, the salesman prepared to leave and handed his new friend and customer a handsome leather memo book with his company's name gold-embossed on it.

"You sure are a nice feller, podner, this is something I can really use."

The salesman then casually asked if he might cash a small check.

Looking the salesman over coldly, the Texan said, "What's that you said, stranger?"

CASH IDENTIFICATION

A sales clerk, accustomed to credit cards, stared stupefied, for a moment, at customer offering cash for his purchase, then suspiciously asked, "You got any identification with you?"

CENTER-FOLD

For years my wife has been complaining she has nothing to wear. I didn't believe her until she showed up in *Playboy* last month!

CHALLENGING TRIP

Sales manager: "Here's a one-way ticket. Land the order and I'll wire you the return fare!"

CHAMPION WANTED

A personnel manager interviewing a prospective salesman wound up with, "What we're looking for is a man of vision, a man with drive, determination and courage; a man who never quits, who can inspire others, in short, a man who can pull the company's bowling team out of last place!"

CHAMPIONSHIP BATTLE

"I remember my wedding day so distinctly," the elderly salesman told the young salesman. "I brought my bride home to the little house I had bought, carried her over the threshold and said, 'Honey, this is your world and this is my world.' "

"And I suppose you both live happily ever after?" queried the younger man.

"Well, not exactly," replied the other grimly. "We've been fighting for the world's championship ever since."

CHANGE OF MANAGEMENT

After the wedding reception the newly wedded businessman replaced the "Just Married" sign on the back of his car, with this sign: "Under New Management."

CHAOTIC SALE

The sales manager was explaining to the new salesman that the former salesman he was replacing had loused up the territory so much that he, the replacement, would experience a most difficult time getting any order out of the chaos.

The new eager salesman replied, "I don't know who this fellow Chaos is, but I'll get an order from him, even if I have to call on him every day for a month!"

CHASING CREDITORS

When the incidental salesman says he has a large following, he usually means that a lot of creditors are trying to catch up with him.

CHEAP FORTUNE-TELLING

The parsimonious executive gave the waitress three new shiny pennies as a tip. The waitress said, "Thank you sir! Now I can tell you what you are. The first penny proves that you're Scotch, the second penny tells me you're a bachelor, and the last penny makes it clear that your father was a bachelor, too!"

CHEATING PERCENTAGE

The salesman was challenged as to how he arrived at the total for his weekly expenses.

He casually explained, "I count the money I have on Monday morning and on Friday night I add what I have left, subtract this from the amount I had on Monday, then, so no one gets cheated, I add 20%."

CHEERS!

One way a sales executive can cheer up his wife is to come home and announce that his secretary is getting married!

CHICKEN TO CHICKS

The Senator liked to dwell on his humble beginnings. He got his start at the $25 a plate dinners and worked up to the $1000 affairs.

CHOICE BUT NOT A CHANCE

Ten year old Joey Hopkins ran the doorbell of a neighbor on his street and when the neighbor answered, Joey excitedly said, "Hi, I'm selling tickets to the Scout's Jamboree, 25¢ each. How many can I put you down for?"

"None," he was told. "I don't believe I'm interested."

Joey scowled, "Your're kidding!"

"No, I'm not."

"I don't suppose you realize that it's guys like you who keep kids like me from making their lousy quotas."

"Well, be that as it may, Joey, I . . . "

"I don't know how guys like you can even shave in the morning!" cried Joey.

"I . . . " started the neighbor.

"Big deal!" interrupted Joey, "always ready to lend a helping hand."

"Well, Joey, I . . . "

Again Joey interrupted with, "The way you act, you'd think I was trying to put the bite on you for fifty dollars instead of a crummy two-bits."

"I'll level with you Joey, the night of your jamboree, we'll be out of town. But, I do want you to know that we'll be with you and your group in spirit!"

"In that case, Mr. Kaiser, where would your spirits like to sit, in the 25¢ seats or the 50¢ seats?"

"O.K., you win, give us two 50¢ seats."

CHOICE OF INTENTIONS

Salesman to a dull boy courting his daughter: "Are your

intentions honorable or dishonorable?"

Boy friend: "Gee, I didn't know I had a choice!"

CHOOSY POOR LUNCHER

An important businessman inspecting a factory site in a run-down neighborhood, was forced to grab lunch in a dirty greasy-spoon diner. He sat down and was amazed to realize that the waiter was a college classmate.

Embarrassed, he said, "Jim, do you work here?"

With a touch of superiority, the waiter replied, "Yeah, but I don't eat here."

CHRISTMAS EDUCATION

This past Christmas I got one of those educational toys. Unfortunately, my wife found out about her.

CHRISTMAS ICICLES

Yesterday I bought my Christmas tree and the attendent said, "Do you have any decorative icicles?"

I answered, "Certainly do, my wife and my secretary!"

CHRISTMAS INSTRUCTIONS

A wife gave her husband simple instructions for buying her Christmas gift. "If you can afford it, forget it!"

CLEANED CLOSING

The salesman didn't suspect how thoroughly buying a home would deplete his savings, until he sat in the loan company office, flanked by a bank officer, real-estate broker, and lawyer.

He was writing and distributing checks as fast as they could explain to whom and for what.

Finally, the loan company's lawyer leaned back and, with a note of concern in his voice, asked, "How do you stand now, financially? Have you any money left?"

"No," he reported, rubbing his hand, which was cramped from writing. "Not a cent!"

"Good," the lawyer said soberly, "Then I haven't made any mistakes."

CLOSING PROBLEM

A salesman, attending a convention, excused himself from the blonde he was drinking with at the hotel bar and went to his sales manager and asked, "Should I take this gal I just picked up to my room or to hers?"

The sales manager replied, "This situation proves that you are certainly skilled in developing an interest, but you are a lousy closer!"

CLOSING THE CLOSER

One day a salesman tried out the "alternate choice" closing technique on his sales manager: "How much of a raise in salary will you give me—$50 or $25?"

The sales manager countered with, "Which do you prefer—to resign or to be fired?"

COAT OF NO RETURN

A woman trying on a mink coat said to the salesgirl, "Now, if my husband doesn't like it, will you promise to refuse to take it back?"

COLD CUT ALLERGY

A salesman's sneeze during a speech on sales promotion, prompted his next seat companion to inquire: "You got the flu?"

The salesman answered, "No, I'm allergic to baloney!"

COLD WAR

We have all the autombiles, but the Communists have all the parking spaces.

COLORFUL BUTTONS

The other day I walked into a car agency to buy a new car. The salesman approached and quickly sized me up.

"You, sir," he declared, "are the sporty type. I know exactly what you want. Take a look at this vehicle. See the buttons on the dashboard? Press the brown one and a brunette jumps into the car. You press the red one and a redhead jumps in. Press the yellow one and a blonde leaps in. Now, sir, do you want to buy this car?"

"Nope," I said, "just the buttons."

COLORFUL CHOICE

One nice thing about this country is that a man can choose his own form of government—blonde, brunette or redhead!

COMMISSION PROBLEM

Now that the troubled salesman was comfortably relaxed on the psychiatrist's couch, he started pouring out his problem.

"Here's my situation. I live in a twenty bedroom house in an exclusive part of Bergen. I have one of the largest swimming pools in my area. Next to it, I have a nine-hole golf course. In addition to all that I own ten automobiles, a cabin cruiser and a twin-engine plane."

"Hold it!" interrupted the headshrinker. "What's your problem?"

"That's my problem, doctor," the salesman answered, "even with commission, I never make more than $100 a week!"

COMPACT FINANCING

Auto salesman to prospect: "This car is so compact that you will need only one finance company to finance it!"

COMPLIMENTS AVAILABLE

Sales manager: "I'd like to compliment you on your fine sales record, Bixby, but when are you going to give me the chance?"

COMPUTERIZED IMPRESSION

Personnel manager to sales applicant: "I can't promise you the job. But our computor is favorably impressed!"

CONSISTENT LOSER

The sales executive was unlucky at his office. He picked losers in the baseball pool and in the secretarial pool!

CONSUMER REPORTS

An appliance shopper asked, "Please, tell me about your electric knives."

The sales clerk, noticing the copy of *Consumer Reports* that the shopper was trying to conceal, replied, "Why don't you tell me?"

CONTEST FOR SURVIVAL

Sales manager: "I'm going to run a little sales contest. The first three winners get to stay with us!"

CONTEST FOR WIFE OF LOSER

Here's the details for an unusual contest: Offer a week-for-two, all-expenses-paid, at a plush resort in Bermuda.

Divide the sales staff into two-men teams, and assign a quota to each man. The man from each team who exceeds established quota by the greatest margin, is the winner of the Bermuda trip—with the wife of the loser!

CONTRIBUTION DENIED

The chairman of a fund drive undertook to solicit a wealthy man who had never contributed. The chairman said, "Our last survey showed you made $90,000 last year. We really hope and feel that you should give something."

The man answered, "Did your survey show that I have a mother with no means of support? Did it show that my sister's husband was killed in a terrible accident, leaving her with four small children? Did it show that my brother was badly injured in World War II? Well, if I don't give to them, why should I give to the fund?"

CONTROLLED DAMAGE

A woman driving for the first time first ran over the kid's bicycle, then she swerved onto the neighbor's lawn, plowed through a hedge, side-swiped a fire hydrant, and then she lost control of the car!

✓ CONVENTION PEACE

"This is the longest convention I ever attended. Two days for travel, three days for meetings, and five days for disturbing the peace!"

CONVENTION PINCHER

In Las Vegas, a salesman and his wife, attending a convention, snuggled into a crowded elevator. The salesman was standing very close to an attractive blonde.

Suddenly, the blonde whirled around and slapped his face. "If there's anything I can't stand," she shouted, "it's a pincher."

When the elevator stopped and the salesman and his wife got out, he said, "That blonde is nuts. I never pinched her."

"I know," said the wife, "I did."

CONVERTED HOMEBODY

After a few years of marriage, the young salesman began to spend many evenings out with other salesmen.

One night his conscience bothered him so he called his wife from his office.

"Hello, darling," he said. "Slip on your party clothes and meet me downtown. We'll have dinner at some quiet place and then we'll see a show. How about it?"

"I'd be delighted to meet you, Bob," she replied, "But why not come out to the house and get me? There's nobody home."

Now, hubby spends every night at home. His name is Henry.

CONVICTION TRANSFERRED

A self-made millionaire proclaimed, "I've always had a theory that salary is the least important part of any job. Doing things whole-heartedly, to the peak of your ability, brings far greater satisfaction than money."

"And you became rich after you convinced yourself that this was true?" he was asked.

"No," corrected the millionaire, "after I convinced the people who worked for me!"

COOLING THE SHOPPER

One Dallas appliance dealer handles the shopper, who is "just looking and wants to visit some other appliance stores" by thanking him for his interest and gives him a little token of his appreciation for coming to his store first.

What is the present? It's a half-gallon of ice cream, and how many stores can you visit with a half-gallon of ice cream under your arm on a hot day in Texas?

COOPERATIVE MATE

It's tough making a go of a marriage if both parties work. Therefore a cooperative husband quit his job.

COST OF BOASTING

The trouble with earning a large salary is that it costs so much to let people know about it!

COST-CUTTING SUGGESTION

The first prize for money-saving ideas and suggestions went to a man who suggested that the award to be cut from $25.00 to $5.00

CREDIT FIRST

The oceanliner was sinking and the passengers were crowding to the lifeboats.

An officer stood on the foredeck and called out above the noise, "Women, children and tourists on the 'Go now, Pay later Plan,' first!"

CREDIT SEARCH

"What a town! I've been in a dozen gin mills and can't get what I want."

"What do you want?" he was asked.

"Credit," was the reply.

CRITICAL SPELLING

Inept salesman to sales manager who had been critical of his selling effort, or lack of selling effort: "I've taken all the criticism that I'm going to take. How do you spell 'Quit'?"

CUSHIONED SPELLING

The executive instructed his secretary to send a letter to a delinquent customer, "Just remind them that their account is three months overdue," he said.

In a few minutes the secretary returned with a letter.

The boss read it and said, "I'm afraid this a little too strong. I don't want to insult them. Just remind them."

A little later he read over the second letter.

"Still a bit vigorous," he explained, "What I want is just to politely remind them they have overlooked paying the bill."

The third letter was prepared. "That's much better," said the executive. "It's just about what I want. Now re-type it and correct two mistakes. There's only one 't' in wretched and one 'i' in swindlers."

CUSTOMER'S ALWAYS WRONG

A salesman decided one day that he had enough of selling. He was going to switch jobs. He became a policeman. A few months later a friend met him pounding his beat and asked how he liked his new job.

"Great!" said the ex-salesman. "What I like best about it is that the customer is always wrong."

CUSTOMERISM

A salesman was asked, "How do you like your new job selling on the road?"

"Oh, it's dandy, you meet some nice fellows at the motels and have lots of fun going out on the town in the evening. But it's a bore calling on those customers the next day!"

D

DADDY'S SCOTCH

After 12 hectic hours as cook, chauffeur, charwoman, and collection volunteer, the harried mother took a sip of Scotch to settle her nerves. She then proceeded to tuck her son into bed.

He looked up at her after she kissed him goodnight, and said, "Mommie, you're wearing Daddy's perfume!"

DANGEROUS DRIVER

An auto dealer equipped a car with a shot-gun in one fender, a machine gun in the other, and a cannon in between. Then he put in the most dangerous weapon of them all—a woman driver.

DATED PAYMENTS

A certain old lady sent every month either too much money or not enough to pay her gas bill. It didn't seem as if she and the gas company would ever agree on how much she owed.

Finally, a kind soul in the gas company wrote a short note to the confused lady: "Please pay the amount at the lower right-hand corner. You have been paying the date in the upper left-hand corner."

DAY AND NIGHT EXTRACTING

A salesman doesn't mind his wife going through his pockets while he's asleep. What bothers him is the way she goes through their bank account while he's awake.

DEAD PRICE

Prospect: "Your price is too high. I can do better."

Salesman: "I don't doubt that. There's always somebody who will come up with a lower price. Let me give you an example.

"A neighbor of mine who needed an operation asked his doctor how much would it cost. The surgeon told him $500. My friend said, 'You'll have to do better than that, I got a much cheaper price from the undertaker.' "

DEAD USED CAR

Used car salesman: "This used car, although it's ten years old, has never been out of the garage. It was owned by a little old lady who used to carbon monoxide husbands."

DEADLY PRESENTATION

I suppose you've heard of the insurance man who lost his job because he talked a customer to death after selling him a life insurance policy!

DEALING HUSBAND

"I just got a Cadillac for my wife."
"Wish I could get a trade like that!"

DECEPTION AT THE DESK

A secretary was named correspondent in a divorce trial of an executive.
Judge: "Miss Smith, did you go to a hotel with the defendant?"
Secretary: "Yes, I did. But I couldn't help it. He deceived me."
Judge: "How did he do that?"
Secretary: "He told the desk clerk that I was his wife!"

DECISION-MAKER

A salesman found he was getting nowhere through the buying office, and asked the receptionist, "If business started going to pot around here, who would yell the loudest?"

The startled young gal named the boss, and the salesman said, "Fine, he's the guy I want to see!"

DECISION PENDING

Door-to-door salesman, to a little girl who had answered the doorbell: "I'd like to speak with the head of the house."

Little girl: "My parents are battling and you'll have to wait until they decide it."

DEDUCTIBLE QUESTION

In a local restaurant, as a salesman paid his check, he turned to the stranger at the next table and asked, "Would you like to buy a hotel?"

The other man said he would not be interested.

"I didn't think you would," the salesman apologized. "I simply mentioned it so I can say that business was discussed at this meal when I report my taxes."

DEFICIENT STOCKHOLDER

One employee to another: "My mistake was buying stock in the company. Now I worry about the lousy work I'm turning out!"

DELAYED LOST FRIEND

Lending money to someone doesn't mean you'll lose him as a friend, it's trying to get it back that will do it!

DELAYED APPRECIATION

. The owner of one of New York's largest department stores was awakened at 3 A.M. in his home by a phone call.

The voice at the other end identified himself, "I'm one of your customers. I bought a sofa in your store, and I want to tell you how beautiful it is."

The sleepy store owner replied, "I appreciate the compliment, but tell me, when did you buy this sofa from us?"

"I bought it from you four months ago."

"What, you bought it from us four months ago and you wake me up at three in the morning to tell me about it?"

"Yes . . . it just arrived!"

DELIGHTED SUBSTITUTE

The pinch-hitter for the scheduled speaker told the audience that finding himself in this unexpected position reminded him of the time when a lady entered her prize male poodle in a dog show. Through some mistake the male poodle was put in competition with a group of female dogs. She was asked: "Did your pet win ribbons?"

"No, he didn't," the lady answered.

"Well, was he commended?"

"No, but he was delighted!"

DEPENDENTS ADDED

I won't say how well I did in the stock market this year, but I've got five new dependents: Merrill, Lynch, Pierce, Fenner & Smith!

DETERMINED DRIVER

"He drove straight to his goal," said the outside speaker. "He looked neither to the right nor to the left, but pressed forward, moved by definite purpose. Neither friend nor foe could delay his course. All who crossed his path did so at their own peril. What would you call such a man?"

"A truck driver," shouted someone from the audience.

DETROIT'S "BUILT-IN"

It's getting harder and harder to find good *used* cars. The cars they make now don't last long enough to become used.

DICTATING FATIGUE

The inept manager had a hard day. He dictated three letters; A, B, and C!

DIETING

"Are you on a diet?" asked the salesman's friend, when he saw him eating milk and crackers.

"No, on commission," was the reply.

DIPLOMACY

The successful salesman diplomatically tells the P.A. he has an open mind, instead of telling him he has a *hole in his head.*

DIRTY CUSTOMERS

At a recent rock festival in Connecticut the local store was mobbed with youthful customers. During that week-end it sold 75,000 cases of beer, 100,000 cans of soup, 200,000 hot dogs and only one bar of soap.

DISAPPROVAL

A henpecked husband finally got fed up with his wife's insistance that he accompany her when she shopped for clothes.

In a crowded lingerie department she held up the briefest of panties and asked if he liked them.

His answer ended his shopping excursions. "I certainly do!" he answered loudly, "but I don't think your husband would approve of them!"

DISLIKES WIFE'S LIP SERVICE

The traveling salesman was asked why he had his wife with him on all his selling trips.

The salesman quickly answered, "I'd rather bring her with me than to have to kiss her good-bye!"

DIVIDED HAPPINESS

Salesman to a friend: "My wife and I have been happily married for 15 years. As a matter of fact, we go out once a week, have steak, champagne and dance.

Envious friend: "That's marvelous!"

Salesman: "It certainly is! My wife goes on Mondays and I go out on Thursdays."

DO IT YOURSELF

The sales speaker stopped his speaking abruptly and pointed to one of the salesman in the audience and appealed to him to wake up the salesman sitting next to him.

The salesman shook his head and retorted, "You do it. You put him to sleep!"

DO NOT DISTURB

An average salesman pleaded with the auto dealer, "I don't care what you do about the commission scale, but please don't mess up my draw."

DOLLAR-LESS EFFORT

The reason a dollar won't do as much for people as it once did is that people won't do as much for a dollar as they once did!

DOMINATING WIFE

Prospect: "I've come back to buy that car you showed me yesterday."

Salesman: "That's fine, tell me, what dominant feature made you decide to buy this car?"

Prospect: "My wife."

DOOR-TO-DOOR WEALTH

A man grumbled that his wife is an easy mark for door-to-door salesmen. "We own everything in the world that costs only $5 a week."

DON'T BE SPELL-BOUND

Preceding the "outside speaker" on the platform, was the vice-president in charge of production, who addressed the salesman's convention on the subject of WORK. He explained that "W" stood for wealth, "O" for orderliness, "R" for right approach to job, and "K" meant job knowledge.

After he had concluded, the director of sales introduced the "Outside speaker" to the bored audience, saying that his topic would be SUCCESSFUL SALESMANSHIP.

A salesman from the back of the room shouted out loud and clear, "O.K. Charlie, but don't spell it out!"

DO'S AND DON'T'S

The salesman was evaluating the new car he had just bought. "The horn doesn't blow, but the tires do. The convertible top doesn't collapse, but the steering wheel does. The engine doesn't start, but the monthly payments have."

DOUBLE-ENTRY

Did you hear about the income-tax cheater who was tripped up by his own stupid mistake? Under Business Expense, he listed his *other set of books.*

DOUBLE LIFE

Suit salesman: "This suit is 200% wool!"
Customer in disbelief: "How come that it is more than 100%?"
Suit salesman: "The sheep that supplied the wool led double lives!"

DOUBLE VISION

Drinking might shorten a man's life, but at least he sees twice as much in the same length of time!

If he drinks Bloody Marys with carrot juice, he'll get just as drunk, but he'll be able to see twice as much!

DOUBT

Salesman: "Are you sure your boss isn't in his office?"
Receptionist: "Are you doubting his word?"

DOWN-HILL PAYMENTS

The sporting goods salesman told the beginning skier who was about to buy a pair of skis on a weekly payment plan, "Don't worry about the payments. Your hospitalization insurance payments will take care of them.

DOWNWARD LOOKS

One trouble with those daring necklines on dresses is that it makes it harder to remember faces. As a matter of fact, it makes you want to "glance all night."

"DRINKS ON ME"

A castaway was washed ashore after many days on the open sea. The island on which he landed was populated by savage cannibals who tied him, dazed and exhausted, to a thick stake. They then proceeded to cut his arms with their spears and drank his blood.

This continued for several days until the castaway could stand no more. He yelled for the cannibal king and declared: "You can kill me if you want to, but this torture with spears has got to stop. I'm tired of being stuck for the drinks!"

DROP-OUT

Did you hear about the inept salesman who wanted to be a drop-out so he burned his business card!

DRUM MAJOR

The sales manager had an annoying habit. He was always drumming his fingers on something. Once his secretary quit because of his drumming. She claimed it put runs in her stockings.

DRY VOTER

During the recent primary elections in California, a drunk walked into a voting booth, closed the curtain and proceeded to take off all his clothes. After he had been in the booth for about 30 minutes, one of the voters waiting in line, yelled to him through the curtain: "Hey, c'mon. Hurry up and vote!"

"Vote?" hollered the confused inebriate, "I'm trying to take a shower!"

DUAL JUMP

A sales executive started across a bridge, when his eye caught a well-dressed man toss a briefcase over the rail and start to climb the barrier. The sales executive raced up to the man and shouted, "Don't do it! Talk about it first."

"What's to talk about?" asked the man bent on suicide. "The world situation has deteriorated to the point where we'll all be blown up soon anyway. Sales of my company are down to the point where I'll have to lay off three quarters of my staff to meet bank notes. What's there to talk about?"

"Look," said the sales exec, "I've plenty of business problems, too, and this world isn't such a bad place to be." On and on talked the sales exec for a full 45 minutes.

And then they both jumped off the bridge.

DUAL ORDERS

The inept salesman reported to his sales manager, "I got two orders today—'Get out,' and 'Stay out!' "

DUSTY CLUE

Housewife: "I don't need a dictionary. I already have one. It's over on the end table over there."

Salesman: "Sorry, I don't believe that's a dictionary, it looks more like a Bible."

Housewife: "How did you figure that out?"

Salesman: "By all the dust on it!"

E

EARLY RETIREMENT

When you realize how little inept salesmen produce, you wonder what they will do when they retire, or are they already retired and don't know it?

It's been said that some inept salesmen die at the age of

thirty but remain on the payroll and are not buried until they reach the age of 65.

EARS TO THE GROUND

At one time, a fellow with his ear to the ground was a politician. Now he's just somebody looking for a lost contact lens.

If you think politics is easy, try straddling a fence while keeping one ear to the ground.

EASIER COMMUNICATIONS

Husband: "This wife of mine spends so much money that it's driving me crazy!"

Neighbor: "Why don't you talk to her about it?"

Husband: "To tell you the truth, it's easier to talk to the creditors."

EDUCATED ROOMMATE

"Sorry, sir," said the hotel desk clerk to the traveling salesman, "but we have no rooms at all, unless . . . "

"Unless what?"

"Unless you'd be willing to share a bedroom with a red-headed school teacher."

"Look," said the salesman, "I know you've heard stories about traveling salesmen, but I'll have you know that I'm a happily married church-going, home-loving man!"

"Well," said the clerk, "so is he!"

EFFORTLESS JOB

A college senior was asked if he was looking for work. He answered, "Not necessarily, but I would like a position."

EIGHTEEN FILLED HOLES

A patient phoned his dentist for an appointment. "So sorry," said the dentist, "not today. I have eighteen cavities to fill." Whereupon he hung up the receiver, picked up his golf bag, and departed.

ELECTRIC BLANKET CALL

An executive's wife called her husband's office and said to his secretary, "I'm at the airport and am flying to Miami for a few days. Will you tell Mr. Maxwell that I forgot to turn off the electric blanket on his side of the bed this morning?"

"Yes, I'll tell him," the secretary replied, "and who shall I say called?"

ELECTROCUTION AT THE OFFICE

Executive: "I've gotten her, my bumbling secretary, an electric typewriter. Next week I'm gonna get her a chair to match."

ELECTRONIC REPLACEMENT

An inept executive, after being fired, said to his wife, "What hurts is that I wasn't replaced by a whole computer, just a transistor."

EMPATHIC EXIT

A salesman was bragging to a purchasing agent that he was calling on: "The reason that I am top producer is because I have empathy with my customers. I have a keen sensitivity of what is in the customer's mind. As an example," he continued, "I know just what you are thinking."

Purchasing agent: "Good, then why don't you get out of here!"

EMOTIONAL APPROACH

If you really want to upset a girl, invite her up to your apartment. Turn down the lights. Put the soft music on the stereo. Pour champagne for two, sit beside her on the couch, take her hand and in a voice throbbing with emotion, try to sell her a Mutual Fund!

EMPTY DEMANDS

The salesman was telling the office manager how his wife was always demanding money from him.

Salesman: "Two weeks ago she wanted $150. Last week she asked for $175. Yesterday she wanted a $100.

Office manager: "What does your wife do with all that money?"

Salesman: "I don't know. I never give her any."

ENCOURAGEMENT

A beautiful young thing walked into a man's store and asked the salesman, "What do you give a man who has everything?"

The salesman, after thinking a second, replied, "Encouragement, gal, encouragement!"

END OF THE LINE

There was a long line waiting in the early morning in front of a clothing store that had advertised a special sale. A man walked to the front of the line. The people grabbed him and pushed him to the end. Again, he walked to the front, and they beat him up and shoved him to the back. Once more, he headed for the front of the line, and they kicked him and pushed him into the gutter. Finally, he got up, brushed himself off, and said to a man at the end of the line, "If they do that once more, I'm not opening the store!"

ENTERTAINED FEE

The program chairman asked a nationally known speaker, "What is your fee?"

The speaker replied, "$300 if I'm not entertained, $500 if I am."

EQUAL OPPORTUNITY

A clergyman was asked if the fighter would benefit by the little prayer he said before the bell rang.

"It will help him, if he can fight. After all, the other fellow also can pray!"

EQUAL RIGHTS

A man called an office-machine salesman, "I would like to have a copying machine delivered to me, and if it is any good, I'll send you a check."

Answered the office machine salesman, "Send us your check and if it is any good we will deliver the copier."

ERRANT RETURN

A bachelor sales executive listed a dependent son on his income tax return. IRS returned it with a notation, "This must be a stenographic error."

He replied immediately, "You're telling me!"

ETERNAL MILITARY DISCOURSE

The toastmaster commented, after lengthy talks by generals and admirals, "Now I know what they mean when they say 'The Army and Navy Forever.'"

EXAMPLE MISSING

Executive to new secretary: "You're twenty minutes late again, don't you know what time we start work in this office?"

Secretary: "Well, er . . . no sir. They're always working when I get here."

EXASPERATED SALESMAN

A woman was buying luggage for her husband. She kept coming back to a case made of alligator hide. Finally, she asked for the third time, "Are you sure this is alligator skin?"

"Positive," asserted the salesman, "in fact, I shot the alligator myself."

The woman shopper queried, "That leather seems rather scuffed-up on this side."

"That," the exasperated salesman blurted, "is where it struck the ground when it fell out of the tree."

EXECUTIVE INDECISIVENESS

An executive, we're told, is someone who knows how to be indecisive in a forceful manner. He thinks twice before saying nothing. He is someone who is able to think a problem over for a few days before he makes a snap decision. Once he makes up his mind, he's full of indecisions. The only time he makes a decision for himself is when he rings for an elevator.

EXECUTIVE PROCASTINATOR

The typical executive is one who won't hesitate to put off 'till tomorrow what his assistant is too busy to do for him today.

EXOTIC AGITATOR

A manufacturer and his wife were watching an exotic dance and the executive wasn't missing any of the dancer's exciting moves.

"Well John," interrupted his wife, "I'm glad to see that something can take your mind off your factory."

"Please," he muttered, not taking his eye off the gyrations, "I've got an idea for a new type of agitator for our next washing machine model!"

EXPEDITIOUS LETTER

One day a certain sales executive had one of the secretaries sitting comfortably on his lap when he espied, through the window of his office partition, his wife approaching.

As she entered the door he began to dictate rapidly, "Take this letter to A.B.C. Furniture Co. 'Shortages or no shortages, how long do you think I can run my office with only one chair?' "

EXPENSE ACCOUNT DECEIVABLE

She was "Honeychile" in New Orleans, the hottest of the bunch; but on the old expense account "she" became gas, cigars and lunch!

EXPENSIVE COMPLAINING

This is the only country in the world where businessmen get together over $20 luncheons to complain about the economy.

EXPENSIVE HAIR

The salesman was fired because the boss found a blond hair on his expense account.

EXPENSIVE HATE

A young man came into the gift store and asked the clerk to show him some expensive gifts. After being shown a variety of expensive gifts he said, "No, none of these will do. I want something even more expensive. It's for my uncle and today is his birthday."

Finally he saw what he wanted, priced right and he bought it.

The clerk asked, "Will you take it with you or shall we send it?"

The nephew replied, "Deliver it. I don't speak to my no-good uncle."

EXPENSIVE MILES

Sales manager: "No wonder you can't find time to eat, sleep and call on prospects. Look at all the miles you have driven according to your expense account!"

EXPERIENCED LEMON PICKER

In desperate straits, a man went to an employment agency seeking a job—any kind of job.

During the interview, the manager of the agency took a paper from his filing cabinet, turned to the applicant and said, "Now if you like to travel, I have a job open in Florida. Can you pick lemons?"

"Can I!" shouted the applicant with excitement, "I've been married five times!"

EXPERIENCED AT NOTHING

First executive: "I remember your son, Mark, was trying so hard to get a job with the federal government. What is he doing now?"

Second executive: "Nothing, he got the job."

First executive: "Then they won't have to break him in!"

EXPLOITED STRIKERS

Striker #1: "We gotta put an end to this exploitation by the robber barons of industry, flim-flamming the working man out of the rightful fruits of his labor. I'm going down to the union hall and vote, 'Strike'!"

Striker #2: "Me too! Shall we take my Cadillac or your Jaguar?"

EXPLOSIVE SALESMAN

The aggressive salesman opened his sales presentation to the production manager saying, "I'd like the opportunity to talk to your employees and prove to them how my motivational course will put fire and sparkle into their work."

The startled manager roared, "Get out of here this second! This is a gunpowder factory!"

EXTENSIVE PRICE

A salesman who is a buff on classic autos bought a car that runs entirely on electricity. It cost him $12,000—$6,000 for the car and $6,000 for the extension cord.

EXTINGUISHER TO GO

The fire-extinguisher salesman was concluding his sales talk to an about-to-be-retired businessman by saying, "This fire-extinguisher is guaranteed to give more than fifty years of service."

The retiring businessman retorted, "That doesn't mean anything to me, since I won't be here very long."

The salesman replied, "In that case, take it with you when you go."

EXTRA-CURRICULAR

A certain secretary went to a wonderful secretarial school. She majored in coffee breaks, long lunch hours, water cooler conversations and collection training.

EYEBALL EXCUSE

The executive's new girl friend was named Daisy Deboys. Now he can look at his wife straight in the eye and say, "Dear, I'm going out with Deboys!"

F

FACSIMILE

An eleven year old boy, after listening to his dad tell him about the birds and the bees said, "You know Dad, the process you described isn't too dissimilar to human reproduction!"

FAIR EXCHANGE

We have a new trade agreement with Russia. We will send them 3000 autos from Detroit and they will send us 20,000 parking spaces from Sibera.

FAIRWAY DATE

Executive: "So you played golf with your salesman friend yesterday. How does he use the woods?"
Secretary: "I don't know, we played golf all the time."

FALSE MORALS

Asked to state his capabilities as a salesman, the applicant said, "Sir, I can sell anything. I enjoy my work. Hours mean nothing to me. Money isn't all important either. I have been highly successful in every sales job I've ever had."
The sales manager inquired, "Do you drink?"
"No sir, never touch it."
"Do you smoke?"
"I cut it out years ago."
"Do you chase women?"
"Heck, no. I'm happily married man, with four children."

Finally the higly impressed sales manager asked, "Don't you have any bad characteristics?"

"Yes, I do," confessed the salesman, "I'm the biggest liar you ever met."

FAME IN WASHINGTON

Three small businessmen were sitting around trying to put a definition on the word "fame."

"Fame," said one, "is being invited to the White House for a talk on business conditions with the President."

"No," said the second, "Fame is when you're at the White House to talk about business conditions, and when the Hot Line rings, the President is too interested in your analysis to let the call interrupt."

The third man said, "You're both wrong. Fame is when you're discussing business conditions with the President, the Hot Line rings and the President answers. The President listens a minute and says, 'Here, it's for you'!"

FAMILIARITY BREEDS FORGETFULNESS

A golf nut at the Concord Hotel played 18 holes and then met his wife at the bar. She wanted to know what happened to their son. The golfer admitted that he hadn't even thought of the youngster for hours.

"But he caddied for you all afternoon," shouted his distraught wife.

"You know," said hubby, "I thought that kid looked familiar!"

FARMER'S SON?

Two salesmen were talking about the Women's Liberation Movement.

"They won't affect us," said one.

"How do you figure that out?" asked the other.

"Because," explained the first salesman. "Who ever heard of a traveling saleswoman joke?"

FASHION PLATE ROBBER

Did you hear about this bankteller who had been robbed three times by the same man? Asked by the police, if she had noticed anything about the thief, she said, "Yes. He seemed to be better dressed each time!"

FAST BASICS

The head football coach gathered his pro team around him for the opening coaching session. "I know that you have all had many years of football experience," he said, "but a review of basic fundamentals is good for everyone now and then."

The coach picked up a football, held it over his head. "Let's start at the beginning. This is a football," he said, extending the ball towards the group. "We play this game on a field which is 100 yards long."

At this point a voice from the back row was heard. "Wait a minute, coach, you're going too fast!"

FAT QUOTES

One hefty executive was quoted as saying: "I have tremendous will power. I force myself to give up trying to diet. Yet, I'm doing something about my weight. I'm keeping it down to my stomach."

FERVID EXECUTIVE

After a complete physical checkup, the 72-year-old executive confided to his physician, "I'm about to marry a lovely 24-year-old girl."

"That could be fatal," counseled the doctor.

"So, she dies, she dies!"

FEWER REFUSALS

A motel owner in the South was complaining to a friend one day about the way his business had fallen off and explained that it was due to a new turnpike that was built about a mile from his place.

But the friend remarked that every time he drove past the motel, he always saw the "No Vacancy" sign out in front, and that looked like a full house.

"Yeah?" snapped the motel man. "Before they opened the new turnpike, I used to turn away 20 or 30 salesmen a night. Now I'm lucky if I have to refuse 10 or 12."

FICTION RIGHTS

"Joe Salesman, if I approve this expense account of yours, will you sign over the fiction rights to it?"

FICTION WRITER

President: "Where is that marketing report I asked you for last week?"

Sales executive: "It takes time to write fiction!"

FILL THE BRIBE

The lingerie sales executive was trying to get the radio personality into plugging his products.

"I'll send you one of our finest and flimsiest negligees. How's that?"

The radio celeb replied, "That all depends on what's-in-it for me."

FINAL STATEMENT

A wife just got a letter from her bank saying: "This is the last time we will spend 8¢ to let you know you have 3¢ in your account."

FINANCED DETERMINATION

A Broadway producer of plays was interviewed on television. He was asked to tell the story of his success.

"I was a struggling young beginner," he explained. "Trying to get my first hit on the boards was a monumental job. I was surrounded by depression, discouragement, mounting bills, all sorts of obstacles. It would have broken any man's back. The weight I carried on my shoulders was an awful responsibility!

"But did I quit? Did I falter? Did I turn and run tail? Heck no! I just gritted my teeth, rolled up my sleeves, raced into a nearby phone booth, called my father and asked for another $100,000!"

FINANCING THE FINANCING

"Just give me one good reason why you can't buy a new car now."

"Well, I'll tell you, man, I'm still paying installments on the car I swapped for the car I traded in as part payment on the car I own now."

FINISHED BUT STILL ON

Someone asked the man who had just left the meeting room if the speaker was finished yet.

"Yes, he finished his speech shortly after he started, but he hasn't stopped talking yet."

FIREWATER

A drunken driver was driving along merrily the wrong way down a one-way street, until stopped by a patrolman.

Cop: "Didn't you see the arrows?"

Drunk: "The arrows? I didn't even see the Indians!"

FIRST THING FIRST

A hold-up man came into a hardware store and pointed a pistol at the clerk.

Clerk: "All right, what do you want?"

Crook: "Well, first I need some bullets for this gun."

Clerk: "You mean it's empty?"

Crook: "No, but it will be in a minute and I'll need some more then."

FIVE DOOR OPENERS

Prospect to a door-to-door salesman: "To what do you owe your extraordinary success as a door-to-door salesman?"

Salesman: "To the first five words I say when a woman opens the door—'Miss, is your mother in?' "

FIVE MINUTE HIT

Lodge member: "The speaker at our lodge dinner to-night was a big hit!"

Wife: "What did he talk about?"

Lodge member: "About five minutes!"

FLAT APPEAL

I know so little about fixing cars that when I get a flat tire, I immediately put up a "For Sale" sign.

FLIGHT COMMUNICATIONS

During a night flight to Australia the airline's Australian pilot inadvertently flicked on the "cabin broadcast" switch. As the coast came into view in the dawn, the passengers heard him say to the co-pilot, "What I need most now is Sheila and an ice-cold beer!"

The stewardess immediately left her cabin in the tail to warn him that the microphone was "live."

As she hurried up the aisle towards the cockpit, a passenger called out, "Don't forget his ice-cold beer!"

FLIGHT PAY-OFF

A traveling salesman, before flight time, stepped on a weight machine that issues fortune cards and upon reading his card, he turned white.

The card said: "Your recent investment will soon pay off!"

FLOORED LIMIT

Two drunks were seated at a bar. One tilted his head back for the next drink and fell off the stool.

His friend, seeing him flat on his back on the floor, said, "That's what I like about Tommy. He knows when he's had enough."

FOAMY HEAD

"Are you the head of this house?" the salesman asked the man at the door, who was drinking a can of beer.

The beer drinker replied, "You bet I am, my wife's gone to bingo!"

FOOLISH TO LISTEN

A customer at the bar was getting drunker and noisier until the bartender had to warn him to quiet down.

"Don't be fussy," said the customer, "this is my 30th wedding anniversary."

"Oh well," said the bartender, "go ahead and enjoy yourself. That certainly calls for a celebration!"

"No, you don't understand," said the customer. "I'm not celebrating. I'm drowning my sorrows."

"Whatever for?" asked the bartender.

"Well, you see, after I was married five years, I was ready to murder my wife. But my lawyer was a friend and he persuaded me not to. He said the least I could get was 25 years in jail. And I was foolish enough to listen to him. Think of it! If I'd gone ahead with it, I'd be a free man today!"

FOLLOW-THROUGH

An inept salesman following-up an inquiry hadn't noticed that it also stated that no salesman should call.

Prospect: "I definitely said 'No Salesman!' "
Salesman: "I'm the closest thing to No Salesman."

FOOTLOOSE DELEGATE

Young son: "It says here in the paper that Mr. Smith went to the convention as a 'delegate at large.' What does that mean?"
Father: "It means he didn't take Mrs. Smith."

FORD HAS A BETTER IDEA

Two Hollywood producers who had never played golf decided to try the game. At the clubhouse of a famous Palm Spring course, they were informed that they couldn't play on the particular afternoon that they had picked for their initial experience with the game.

"Why not?" they demanded indignantly.

"Because," the pro explained, "there are no caddies."

The two producers pondered this for a moment. Then one said, "So who cares? For one afternoon, we can take a Mustang."

FOREIGN LOSERS?

Two foreign industrialists met. The German industrialist said, "Today, Germany is the strongest nation in Europe."

The Japanese industrialist said, "Today, Japan is the strongest nation in Asia."

The German thought for a moment, and said, "I wonder how the winners are doing?"

FORGETFUL SALESMAN

The sales manager was telling his assistant, "You know our city salesman, Oscar, can't remember anything. I just sent him out for a package of cigars for me and I'll bet you, he will even forget to come back."

Just then Oscar came into the office. "Mr. Kaiser, you'll never guess what happened to me an hour ago. I stopped in to see the buyer at XYC Company, who has never bought anything from us, and sold him a 12 gross order!"

The sales manager disgusted, said, "See, he forgot the cigars!"

"FORGET THE TIPS"

The manager sought out his second basemen in the locker room. "Billy," he said, "remember all those batting tips, double-play pivots and base-running hints I gave you this afternoon?"

"Sure, skipper," said the player enthusiastically.

"Forget 'em," murmured the manager. "We just traded you to Philadelphia."

FORGETTING TO REMEMBER

Inept salesman to prospect: "Please won't you let me give my complete sales talk? It's getting so that I am beginning to forget the close."

FORGOTTEN REMEMBRANCE

A salesman whose garage daily delivers his car, found one December morning, a card on the front seat which read: "Merry Christmas from the boys in the garage."

He had every intention of sending a fitting remembrance to his friends in the garage, with his best wishes, but before he got to doing it, he was favored with another card: "Merry Christmas. Second notice."

FORTUNE TO SHARE

A salesman called on my wife the other day and tried to sell her a freezer.

"You'll save a fortune on your food bills," he promised. "I can't tell you how much you'll save. It'll be tremendous!"

Said my wife, "I'm sure you're right, but we're already saving a fortune with our new car by not taking a bus. We're saving a fortune with our new washing machine by not sending out the laundry. We're saving a fortune with our new dishwasher by giving up the maid. The plain truth is that right now we just can't afford to save any more!"

FOUR-LETTER WORD

One inept salesman had a hang-up on a four-letter word: "Work." He heard that hard work never killed anybody, but he's not taking any chances on being the first victim.

He's not afraid of hard work, he's fought it successfully for years!

FOUR "NOS" AND A "YES"

The bank supply salesman was making out an order with the vice-president of a bank when the phone rang. The vice-president's telephone conversation went like this: "No . . . no . . . no . . . yes . . . no . . . ."

The salesman was intrigued with what he had heard and asked the banker what the lone "yes" was for.

The banker replied, "He wanted to know if I could hear him!"

FRANCHISE FORTUNE

Recently at a Harvard Business School session on motivation, so the story goes, a young executive rose to his feet and described a chicken and a pig walking on a country lane.

"The chicken," he said, "excitedly told the portly pig of his new business idea. 'We'll prepare and franchise the best tasting ham and eggs that money can buy, and we'll make a fortune!'

'Wait a minute,' said the portly pig. 'It's easy for you to get enthused; for you it's just a contribution, but for me, it means total commitment!' "

FREE-LOADING SIDE

The bartender was asked, "Do you drink while on duty?"

To which he replied, "Yes, I can't afford it when I'm on the customer's side of the bar."

FRESH POWER

A young and eager real estate salesman handled the objection of an unsightly electric substation that was next door to a house that he was trying to sell, by saying, "But, being this close, your electricity will always be fresh!"

FRESH SALESMANSHIP

Young housewife: "Are those eggs strictly fresh?"

Grocer to clerk: "Feel of those eggs, Henry, and see if they're cool enough to sell yet."

FRIENDLY SALES

A man went to buy an overcoat from a clothing dealer who was a neighbor of his. The price was rather high, but he liked the coat. So he appealed to the dealer. "Well, it's a smart coat, but since we are such good friends, couldn't you give me a better price?"

The dealer replied, "Sure we're friends. And it's from my friends that I make a living. My enemies don't even come into my store."

FRIGHTFUL FASHIONS

Clerk to a customer in a dress shop: "But Madam, looking ridiculous is the fashion this year!"

FROM THE TOP

Unemployed man: "How about a job in this store as a salesman?"

Clothing store owner: "No sir! In this store you don't start at the top. First, you have to start as a partner."

FRUGAL EXECUTIVE

One executive dictates with two secretaries on his lap in order to avoid the expense of buying carbon paper!

FUNNY AMERICANS

You know, we Americans sure are funny people. We took the country away from the Indians who scalped us, and then turned it over to the politicians, who skin us!

FUTILITY OF EARNINGS

Do you know, with money so hard to get, and still harder to keep, that it's downright astonishing that anybody would be foolish enough to work for the stuff!

FUTURE THANK YOU

Boss: "Yes, Sylvester, I know you can't get married on the salary I'm paying you, and some day you'll thank me for it!"

G

GARBAGE DISPOSAL FOR MONEY

A salesman handed a New York cab driver a five dollar bill and asked for change.

The cabbie replied, "Here in New York a five dollar bill is change!"

GAY LIBERATION

A pretty young girl came over here from Italy and obtained a job with a leading ad agency. She was brilliant, but word got around the office, eventually to her boss, that she liked girls, not boys.

The boss called her in and said, "Miss Giovanni, you have a fine creative mind and there's no telling how far you can go in this agency, but there's something about your private life which has to be corrected. Now my best advice to you, is to meet a nice young man and get married."

Three days later she met a tall, blond young Australian man and the next day they got married.

The first, second and third nights passed—no action.

They separated and so-o-o, she went back to Florence and he went back to Sydney!

GENEROUSLY DENIED

The business had prospered exceedingly well and the owner now had enough to buy anything he wanted.

One day his secretary brought in some fat checks for him to sign: $150,000 for his new suburban home, $90,000 for a new yacht, and $60,000 for his daughter's wedding.

After signing the checks and handing them back to his secretary she said, "By the way, I've been working for you for over five years and at this time, I'd appreciate a $10 raise."

The astonished executive cried, "$10 raise! What do you think I am, a millionaire?"

GENTLY OFF

Auto salesman: "This foreign model has a top speed of 155 miles per hour and she'll stop on a dime!"

Prospect: "What happens then?"

Salesman: "A small putty knife emerges and scrapes you gently off the windshield."

G. I. ORDERTAKER

Sergeant: "Soldier, what was your occupation before being drafted?"

Soldier: "Salesman."

Sergeant: "Good, you'll get plenty of orders here!"

GIFT FOR PROTECTION

You know what to give a secretary who has everything? A police whistle!

GIFT OF CONSCIENCE

An eager-beaver salesman was trying to have a country store-keeper carry his product, and finally tried to bribe the fellow with a bottle of champagne.

"Oh, my conscience wouldn't let me take a gift," the merchant protested.

"What if I sell it to you for a dime?" asked the salesman.

"In that case," replied the merchant, "I'll take two."

GLAMOR HATS

A wife with an armful of new hat boxes, greeted her husband upon her return from shopping; "A saleslady in Macy's hat department couldn't understand why a glamorous woman like myself wasn't on the stage!"

GOING PLACES?

If an inept salesman say's he is going places, it doesn't necessarily mean he's ambitious. It may mean his wife is out of town!

GOLFER'S LAMENT

A golfer at a 19th hole bar, said to his playing partner, "My wife told me this morning that she is going to leave me if I don't give up playing golf. I'm certainly going to miss her!"

GOOD AS NEW

"Mummy, what becomes of an automobile, when it gets too old to run any more?" asked a little girl.

"Why, my dear," replied mother, "someone sells it to your father as a second car—a great used car—as good as new!"

GOOD OLD PRICES

The inexperienced sales clerk asked the buyer, "How do I handle customers who compare our price today, with the low prices of what they call, the 'good old days'?"

"Be astonished," the buyer replied, "and say 'I didn't think you were old enough to remember those days'!"

GRADUATED CLOSE

Business-school salesman, at the close of his sales presentation:
"Write your name on this line, just the way you want it to read on
your diploma."

GRAFFITI

When a secretary can read the handwriting on the wall, she's in
the wrong rest room.

GREEN STAMP STRATEGY

A woman bought $2000 worth of presents and the next day got
her money back. Then she bought $4000 and then $6000 of
presents, and the next day got her money back.

I asked, "What's the point?"

She replied, "The green stamps you keep!"

GRIDIRON CONSPIRACY

One high school football coach has such a tremendous inferior-
ity complex that every time the team goes into a huddle, he's sure
they're talking about him.

GROUNDED EXCUSE

The sales executive was extremely upset to arrive at the
boarding gate and see his flight taxiing for take-off.

He turned to his wife, who was accompanying him on this
particular business trip, and angrily said, "If you hadn't taken so
long, we wouldn't have missed this plane."

She rebuffed: "If you hadn't rushed me so, we wouldn't have so
long to wait for the next flight!"

GROUP AFFAIR

A jealous executive dictated the following letter to a salesman
he suspected had become too friendly with his wife: "Dear Sir; It
has been called to my attention that for some time you have been
carrying on an affair with my wife. So that we can settle this
matter intelligently, please be in my office at three P.M. on
Friday."

He received this short reply from the salesman: "Dear Sir, I
received your circular letter this morning. You are advised that I
will attend the scheduled conference on time."

GUARANTEED SUCCESS

Where else but in America could a young man start to work in a big factory as a shipping clerk, and two weeks later become a salesman. One month later become a sales manager, six weeks later, junior vice-president in charge of sales, two months later, senior vice-president in charge of productions. And at a board of directors meeting the following month be made senior vice-president, at a salary of $100,000 a year?

It actually happened to a friend of mine. At that board meeting the president of the company shook my friend's hand and asked if he had something to say.

"Thanks," said the new tycoon.

"Is that all you can say?" thundered the president. "This is a momentous day in your life!"

"Yes, that's true," answered my friend, "so tonight I'm going to celebrate. Tell Mom I won't be home for dinner."

GUEST PROOF

Salesman, demonstrating sofa: "Another good feature about it is that when guests arrive unexpectedly, it cannot be turned into a bed!"

GUILTLESS

Secretary: "Doctor, you must help me. I say yes every time, then I feel guilty and depressed."

Doctor: "You want me to strengthen your will power?"

Secretary: "Heavens no! I want you to weaken my conscience!"

GUILTY MINK

Two secretaries arrived in their office one morning. The blonde was wearing a brand new mink coat.

"How do I look?" she asked her friend.

Said the friend, "Guilty."

H

HABIT BREAKING

A man walked up to a cigarette counter and asked for a brand name pack of cigarettes. The clerk questioned whether he wanted the soft pack or crush-proof box? King size or regular size? Filter tip or plain tip? Mentholated or minted? Green pack or blue pack? Seven extra puffs or five extra puffs?

Finally, he asked, "Is this a charge or will you pay cash?"

The exasperated customer exclaimed, "Forget it. I just kicked the habit!"

HALF SCANDALOUS

The executive, traveling by train, had just finished eating in the dining car and had returned to his roommette. He was startled when he walked into the compartment to find two sexy-looking dolls inside. He immediately cried out: "You girls are interlopers! I'm a married man, a pillar of my church, and scandal has never touched my personal deportment. So, one of you girls will have to go!"

HAM ON RYE

A speaker who had bored his audience for almost a half-hour said, "After such a meal as I had this noon, if I had eaten another bite I would be unable to continue speaking."

From the far end of the room came an order to the waiter: "Give him a sandwich!"

HANDICAPPED GOLFER

A golfer having a bad day on the links, went into a tantrum at the last hole. Cussing, he broke up his clubs, moaning over and over, "I've got to give it up. I've got to give it up."

"Give up your golf?" asked the caddy.

"No," he replied, "Give up the ministry!"

HANDICAPPED SHOPPER

A golf widow asked the sporting goods sales clerk, "I'd like a low handicap."

The puzzled sales-clerk repeated, "A low handicap?"

"Yes, a low handicap," the lady affirmed. "It's for my husband's birthday. He's always wishing he had one."

HANDLED WELL

The concerned program chairman tried to hush and quiet down the restless audience while the speaker was droning on and on.

After banging the gavel several times, the end flew off and hit a salesman in the front row. Embarrassed, the chairman apologized. But the salesman responded by saying, "Hit me again, Henry, I can still hear him."

HANDLE WITH CARE

A heavy drinker got on a plane as a passenger, and after more cocktails in flight, got off as baggage.

HAPPY LOSERS

Guests at a recent party dunked for apples in a pail of bourbon. No one won, but you never saw such a bunch of happy losers!

HEAD BUYER

A movie actor newly returned from several months in the Belgian Congo, brought back a trunkful of shrunken heads. Hoping they might be worth something, he called up a well-known department store.

"I would like to speak to someone about the possibility of selling some shrunken heads," he announced.

"One moment please," the switchboard operator replied politely.

In a few minutes he heard a click and a very prim voice say, "Hello, this is the head buyer speaking."

HEAD START

A salesman stopped for a red light and was bumped by the car in the rear. He saw the woman driver in his mirror, turned around and glared at her. At the next light he had to stop short because of jay-walking pedestrians. He was bashed in the back by the same car. He opened his door, leaned out and shouted, "Watch it, please!"

When he stopped for a light at the next corner, he was bumped again. This time, the woman got out of her car and came forward with her license and other identification.

"Look lady," the man pleaded. "I don't want your license or the name of your insurance company. I just want a five-minute head start!"

HEADS OR TAILS

"Moriarty tap the till? I doubt it, but I'll watch him," said Doyle. So he bored a hole in the back door to watch Moriarty.

A customer came in, put down a quarter, and had a drink. Moriarty took the quarter. "If it's heads," he said, "I'll put it in the register, it's Doyles. If it's tails, it's mine. Tails!" So he put it in his pocket.

Two men came in. They put a half dollar on the bar. Moriarty took the half-dollar. "If it's heads, I'll give it to Doyle. Tails, I'll keep it myself. Tails!" Into his pocket it went.

A couple of more patrons came in and ordered drinks. Again Moriarty said, "Tails, I'll keep it; heads I'll give it to Doyle." It came down heads.

"Well," said Moriarty, "I'll make it three out of five." For the third time it came down heads. "Oh well," said Moriarty, "I'll keep it anyway."

"Oh no you don't!" shouted Doyle from behind the door. "Put that in the register! I won that fair and square."

HEAT UTILIZATION

Political conventions should be held during the winter. It's a shame to waste all that hot air!

HEAVENLY DRIVE

She said, "Be an angel, let me drive!"
He did—He is!

HIGH AND LOW PRICING

The used-car dealer was asked, "How come you pay the highest prices for the cars you buy and you get the lowest price for the cars you sell?"

The used car dealer answered, "I don't know, but we must be doing something wrong."

HIGH COST OF LEAVING

When you realize that you never see an undertaker driving a compact car, you know that the high cost of living is not as serious as the high cost of *leaving.*

HIGH-PRICED ECONOMY

New car prospect: "$4,250 is pretty high for a compact car."
Salesman: "Nowadays, if you want economy, you have to pay for it."

HOLDINGS

Last year I put $5,000 into a holding company and I just found out what they're holding—my $5,000!

HOLE IN ONE

The inept salesman was talking about how he got started in sales.

"I started out on the theory that the selling world had an opening for me and it certainly did—I'm in that hole now!"

HOME AT LAST

The tombstone salesman and a widow were discussing what should be inscribed on her late husband's tombstone.

The salesman suggested, "How about 'Gone Home'?"

The Widow replied, "I'll buy that. It's appropriate. Home was always the last place he ever thought of going."

HOME DEMONSTRATION

A salesman came home from selling one day to find his house in a mess.

"What happened?" he exclaimed to his wife.

"You're always wondering what I do all day," she said. "Well, here it is; I didn't do it."

"HOME, JAMES!"

In the midst of one of the wildest parties he'd ever been to, the young salesman noticed a very prim and pretty girl sitting quietly apart from the rest of the revelers.

Approaching her, he introduced himself and said, "I'm afraid you and I don't really fit in with this jaded group. Why don't I take you home?"

"Fine," said the girl, smiling up at him demurely. "Where do you live?"

HOME OFFICE PROXIMITY

Stewardess to nervous Minister: "Would you care for a drink?"
Minister: "No thanks, it's too close to the Home Office!"

HOME SALES ONLY

Vice president: "Is Paul a good salesman?"
Sales manager: "Are you kidding? The only orders he takes are from his wife!"

HOMECOMING ATTRACTION

An automobile salesman drove home in the brand new, bright red promotional car. When his wife saw him drive up in the sporty convertible, she insisted that she be allowed to drive it down to the local shopping center. She returned a half hour later, flustered and annoyed.

"Every truck driver honked his horn and waved at me," she explained to her husband. "Every man on the side walk whistled after me. It was whistles and honking and waving and shouting all the way home."

She turned a deep pink when her husband took her by the hand, led her to the back of the car and showed her the sign: "I don't cost as much as you think!"

HONEST APPEAL

Three men were running in an election for county prosecuter. The incumbent, seeking re-election, was well known and so was one of his opponents. The third man in the race was a young salesman unknown to the electorate generally.

At a rally, the incumbent and the well known opponent proclaimed their respective virtues at great length.

But the salesman in his speech said, "If it weren't for the incompetence of one of my opponents, the other would be in jail!"

He was elected!

HONEST HOUSE

The conscientious congressman held his job uppermost in his heart and mind even while at home.

One night his wife nudged him from his slumber and whispered, "Sam, I think there are burglars in the house."

Sam raised up on one arm, squinted, and replied, "No, my dear. There may be a few in the Senate, but in the House? Never!"

HONEST SILVER SPOON

Heckler: "Yeah, you can talk about Medicare with that silver spoon in your mouth, but your opponent knows what it's like to worry about paying doctor bills every month!"

Candidate: "I can't do anything about my silver spoon, sir, except point out that it enables me to keep my hand out of the public till!"

HORIZONTAL INVITATION

The salesman told his date, "I want you to understand, that when I invite a girl to my apartment to see my etchings, it's usually not a standing invitation."

HOT RING

The sweet young thing had just become engaged. All day she dangled the ring in front of everyone at the office, but to her disappointment, no one noticed it. When work stopped for the afternoon coffee, she made a last desperate effort.

In the loudest voice she could muster, she remarked, "My word, isn't it hot in here? I think I'll take my ring off!"

"HOW DO YOU DO!"

A men's clothing store manager has a foolproof formula for selling suits his clerks cannot move from the racks.

"Here's a new number just imported from Paris," he assures a dubious customer, "that will perk up your appearance so that even your best friends won't recognize you. Just walk around the block in it and see what it does for you."

When the customer comes back, the tailor shakes him by the hand and exclaims, "Good morning, you well-dressed stranger! What can I do for you?"

HUMANE OFFER

A hold-up man, with a seven foot long 2 x 4, handed a teller a note directing him to fill a paper bag with money.

"Get out of here, man," said the teller.

After being hit six times by the hold-up man, with the 2 x 4, the teller shouted, "Okay, quit it. I'll give you the money.

After the hold-up man had pocketed the money and started to leave, the teller called him back, reached in his pocket and handed him $20.

"Why?" the hold-up man asked.

The teller replied, "Go get yourself a gun, you might hurt someone with that thing!"

HUNGRY ROBBER

A supermarket was held up one day. The hold-up men ignored the money in the cash registers at the check-in counters. But did they take a load of groceries!

I

"I SURRENDER DEAR"

A secretary inquired of a salesman, "As you know I'm very popular with you salesmen in this office. Is it because of my face?"

"No."

"My figure?"

"No."

"My sexy personality?"

"No."

"I give up," the secretary said.

"That's it!"

IDEAS FOR UTILIZATION

I like daiquiris. The lime gives me strength, the sugar gives me energy and the rum gives me ideas on what to do with the strength and energy!

ILLEGIBILITY

The executive who has his name printed on company stationary letterheads is not necessarily a "Big Shot." It may be because no one can read his signature.

IMPAIRED DISCERNMENT

Wife: "I could have married a dozen men better than you."

Salesman: "And now I have to suffer for your lack of judgment!"

IMPATIENT RETAILER

A retailer sent an order to a distributor for a sizable amount of goods.

The distributor wired him: "Can't ship until you pay your last consignment."

The retailer's answer, collect, was: "Can't wait that long. Cancel order."

IMPERTINENCE

Salesman: "Although this is one more time that you didn't give me an order, I can say you're not as big a fool as you used to be."
Purchasing agent: "What do you mean by that impertinence?"
Salesman: "You've lost some weight!"

IMPLIED CONSENT

When a customer asks Tony at the fruit counter, "How much for a dozen bananas?" he simply reaches for a paper bag, puts in 12 bananas, hands the bag to the customer and says "60¢"!

IMPORTANT OR UNIMPORTANT

It's amazing how important your job is when you want the day off, and how unimportant it is when you want a raise!

IMPORTED COMPLAINT

The modern American drinks Brazilian coffee from an English cup while sitting on Danish furniture after coming home from an Italian movie in his German car. Then he picks up a Japanese ball-point pen to write a letter to his congressman demanding that something be done about all the gold that's leaving this country.

IMPROVEMENT FUND

Guest speaker: "Please give my fee to your club's favorite charity."
Program chairman: "Good, then we'll put it in our special fund."
Guest Speaker: "What's the purpose of your special fund?"
Chairman: "To help us schedule better speakers next year."

IN AND OUT BANKING

A new drive-in bank opened with twin windows for tellers. Now a man can make a deposit at one, from the front seat of the car, while his wife is making a withdrawal from the rear seat, at the other window!

IN AND OUT CHANCE

The supermarket manager was interviewing a high school student to work in and around the store as a handy-boy.
He told the young fellow, "O.K. you're hired. You'll be working half inside and half outside."

"I'm ready to start," the new handy-boy said, "but what happens to me if a gust of wind should blow the door shut?"

IN SALES NOT MANAGEMENT

The jet liner was on routine flight, but had run into a sudden violent storm. A nice old lady appealed to the minister sitting next to her.

"Please," she said, "I think we're going to crash. Can't you do something to save us?"

"I'm terribly sorry," said the minister, calmly, "but there's not much I can do. You see, I'm in sales, not management!"

INCRIMINATING QUESTION

One secretary was asked how long it takes her to get to work, after she reaches the office.

INDEBTED ANSWER

Executive: "Will you O.K. a loan of $10,000 for me?"
The banker didn't answer.
Executive: "I've just asked you to lend me $10,000."
The banker still remained silent.
Executive: "Why don't you say something, at least you owe me an answer."
Banker: "I'd rather owe you an answer than have you owe me $10,000."

INEXPERIENCED CLOSER

"You haven't been a salesman very long," said a customer in a large department store.

Puzzled, the salesman replied, "How can you tell that madam?"

"You still blush when you quote the prices!" she said.

INFLATED HOTEL BILL

A business executive on an out-of-town sales trip was about to check in at a hotel, when he noticed a lusciously proportioned young woman, smiling at him provocatively. Very casually he walked over to her and spoke a few inaudible words. He returned to the desk with her clinging to his arm and they registered as man and wife.

After a two-day stay, he checked out and was handed a bill for $750.

There's some mistake here," he protested. "I've only been here two days!"

"Yes sir," the clerk explained, "but your wife has been here for two months."

INFLATION CLOSE

A real estate salesman remarked to a young couple wavering on whether to go ahead and buy the house they had just viewed, "It's to your immediate advantage to buy right this minute, because this house is increasing in value every minute you procrastinate."

INITIAL SALE

The head of a big corporation handed out cigars to everybody one morning.

"My son," he exulted, "made his first dollar yesterday since he got out of college six months ago. He sold the watch we gave him for graduation!"

INSECURITY

An insecure executive usually has his name, if not scotch-taped, printed on his office door in chalk, with an eraser hanging on the door knob!

INSIDE SPORT

The executive was so nervous and worried about the speech he had to make that he had butterflies in his stomach. Turning to the meeting chairman, he told him of his nervousness.

The chairman advised, "Here, take this aspirin and the butterflies will go away."

The executive moaned in reply, "I have already taken an aspirin and the butterflies are playing ping-pong with it!"

ISLAND OF SELF INTEREST

The very self-centered executive talking about a convention he attended said, "I would have been terribly bored, were it not for the fact that I was present myself."

INSPIRATION PLUS

At the conclusion of an inspirational sales meeting, the salesman rushed out and hailed a taxi.

When the cab driver asked him, "Where to?"

He replied, "Take me anywhere. I have prospects everywhere!"

INSTANT GENTLEMAN

An executive, who was known for his tactfulness and diplomacy, opened the wrong door in a movie studio that he was visiting, and found the studio's new sex symbol taking a bath.

Quick as a flash he said, "I beg your pardon, Sir!"

In fact, he was such a gentleman, he stood there in the doorway for ten minutes, apologizing!

INSTANT PROSPECT

Husband: "Honey, do you know we have only one more payment on the living room furniture."

Wife: "Great, then we can throw it all out and buy some new stuff."

INSTANT SLOWDOWN

Despite instant coffee machines in sales offices, no one has speeded up the coffee break!

INSTRUCTED WIFE

The executive said to his secretary, "I don't want to see anyone. If anybody says it's urgent, tell them 'That's what they all say.' "

In a few minutes, a lady asked to see "Mr. Exec" and when the secretary repeated her instructions, she was startled to hear, "But I'm his wife."

The secretary then responded, as coached, "That's what they all say!"

INSUFFICIENT REASON

Upon learning that one of her checks had bounced because of insufficient funds, the gal called the bank and advised them, "I'm withdrawing my account from your bank. I'm certainly not going to maintain a checking account in a bank that hasn't sufficient funds!"

INSURANCE

Salesman to his wife: "Honey, I just bought a $100,000 life insurance policy. Now, if anything should happen to me, you and the boys will be taken care of."

Wife: "That's marvelous! Now why don't you go out in the street and play football with the boys."

INSURED BREAK-AWAY

Recently a hold-up robber broke his leg trying to get away from a pursuing policeman. So now he gets workmens compensation for an on-the-job injury.

INTELLECTUAL CLOSE

"What do I need an encyclopedia for?" said the egg-head to the door-to-door salesman, "I'm well informed about everything."

"That's just it," pointed out the salesman, "just imagine the fun you're going to have finding all the errors they made in it!"

INTELLIGENT BACHELORS

A psychiatrist was once asked, "Do intelligent salesmen make good husbands?"

He gave this opinion: "Intelligent salesmen don't get married."

INTERESTING FRIENDS

Don't ever forget that when your friends borrow money from a bank they pay interest.

When they borrow from you, they lose interest.

INTERESTING OBSERVATION

A bank vice-president made this observation, "A woman without principle draws plenty of interest!"

INTERNAL GUESSING

The salesman filed his income tax form and didn't sign it. He reasoned: if they want me to guess how much I made let them guess who sent it.

INVENTORY NOT NECESSARY

After the salesman learned that he was now a new father of quintuplets, his first words to his wife were: "Honey, a sample would have been sufficient. There's no need to carry an inventory."

INVISIBLE SALES

Salesman to lady shopper: "Am I sure these hairnets are invisible? Listen, I sold 3 dozen of them this morning. Yesterday I sold 8 dozen, and between you and me, we haven't had any of them in our store since we ran out of stock and forgot to re-order them three weeks ago!"

I.R.S. COMMUNICATIVE STRATEGY

Before you file your returns, the Internal Revenue Service advises you to call them. But, after you have filed, they tell you, "Don't call us. We will call you."

IRVING GRASSHOPPER

A grasshopper walked into a tavern and hopped up on the bar stool, "I'll have a scotch and soda."

The bartender said, "Did you know we have a drink named after you?"

"Really, you mean you have a drink named 'Irving'?" asked the grasshopper.

ISMS

Socialism is when you have two cows and give one to your neighbor.

Communism is when you have two cows but the government takes both and gives you the milk.

Capitalism is when you have two cows. You sell one and buy a bull. That's free enterprise.

"IT'S A BIG BOY!"

A few days ago a secretary came into the office and began handing out cigars, each tied with a blue ribbon, and small individual boxes of candy, also tied with blue ribbons.

Her co-workers asked the reason for her generosity.

It's a boy!" she beamed, proudly showing off the diamond wedding ring on her finger. "A boy, six feet two, weighting 195 pounds!"

"IT'S FOR YOU"

The new secretary ignored the ringing telephone, and after several minutes of aggravation the sales manager told her to answer it.

"That seems a bit silly," she replied, "because it's bound to be for you. None of my friends know I'm here yet."

J

JABBERING ABOUT UNKNOWN

Gossipy sales clerk: "I won't go into all the details; in fact, I've already told you more about it than I heard myself."

JOINT ACCOUNT

Teller: "What kind of an account do you wish to open?"
Young wife: "Joint. Deposit for him and checking for me!"

JUDGEMENT OF EXPERIENCE

"There's no doubt about it," said a friend to an elderly sage in a small town, "you're the wisest and shrewdest man in these parts. To what would you attribute the fact that you know so much?"

"Good judgment," replied the sage, "I'd say it was my good judgment."

"But where did you get your good judgment?" persisted the friend.

"That I got from experience."

"But where did you get your experience?"

"From my bad judgment."

JUSTIFIABLE ANSWER

Inept salesman: "Will I be getting a raise soon?"
Sales manager: "Of course, you will be getting a raise and it will be effective just as soon as you are."

JUSTIFICATION WANTED

Sales manager to inept salesman: "You told me how good of a salesman you were when I hired you, three months ago. Now tell me all over again, I'm getting discouraged.

JUSTIFY

A mini skirt should be short enough to show she's woman, but long enough to show she's a lady!

JUVENILE CIGAR SMOKER

A door-to-door salesman was amazed to see a nine year old boy, puffing on a long black cigar, answer his ring.

"Good afternoon, sonny, is your mother in?"

"What do you think?"

K

KEPT AUTO

I bought a used car that the salesman bragged was "Garage-Kept."

He was right. The neighborhood garage kept it all the time for repairs!

KEPT SALESMANSHIP

Meek looking customer: "Do you keep razor blades?"

Fresh clerk: "No, we sell 'em!"

Customer walking away: "You'll keep the ones that you might have sold me!"

KIDNAPPED EXCUSE

A salesman, after the sales meeting dinner was over, joined several other salesmen "going out on the town." Before he realized it, it was morning. Being dawn, it dawned upon him that he had better call home with some kind of explanation.

When his wife answered, he put some excitement in his voice and said, "Don't pay the ransom, I escaped!"

KITCHEN TRAITOR

A union official, after an argument with his wife, appealed to a friend to settle the dispute, since words had become hot and heavy. His friend, after listening to the whole story of the argument, sided with the wife.

"So-o-o," screamed the union official, "You've gone over to management!"

KNITTED TRANSPORTATION

A used car prospect said to the salesman, "You call that a bargain? My grandmother could knit a better looking car than that!"

KNOW HIS OWN RISK

The executive had been granted a bank loan the day before. Now he's back in the same bank, withdrawing his account. When he was asked why, he replied, "I don't have confidence in a bank that would lend money to such a poor risk."

KNOWLEDGEABLE GROOMS

The district sales manager warned his new and young encyclopedia salesman: "Never try to sell a set to a bride."
Salesman: "I don't understand, why not?"
Sales Manager: "Brides always think that their husbands know everything."

KNOWLEDGE LIMITED

Charlie was on the job for the first day as a salesman. He was sitting in the sales manager's office waiting for his return from lunch and for further instruction, when the phone rang. Charlie picked it up and said, "Hello."

The company president was on the line and proceeded to ask a long complicated question. When at last he finished, Charlie answered, "Guess I can't help you sir, because when I said 'Hello' I told you everything I understand about this place."

L

LAST CALL

A salesman in Hell recognized the buyer he couldn't see on earth and went up to him and said, "Mr. Purchasing Agent, I'm here for that appointment."

The purchasing agent asked, "What appointment?"

"Why, don't you remember?" the salesman answered, "On every call that I made at your office, you would say 'I'll see you in Hell!' "

LAST CONTRACT

A baseball pitcher once won 20 games in a season for a minor league team that wound up in the cellar. When it came to contract time the following spring, the pitcher complained to the club president because he was offered the same salary.

"You forget that I won 20 games," he pointed out. "And for a last place club, too."

"What difference does that make?" asked the boss. "We could have finished last without you!"

LAST LAUGH

At the end of his first day on the job, a new salesman inquired of the bookkeeper, "Doesn't that sales manager of ours ever laugh out loud?"

"Only," sighed the bookkeeper, "when we ask him for a raise."

LAST OF THE MONOTONY

The morning session of the third day of a tiring convention was over and the crowd was slowly coming back from lunch. Two men sat in the first row and waited and waited. Finally one turned to the other and asked, "Are you going to stay until the bitter end?"

Replied the second man, who just happened to be the afternoon speaker, "Friend, I am the bitter end."

LAST ORDERS

A timid salesman was advised by a psychiatrist to toughen up at home. That evening, this ordinarily quiet guy told his wife she was taking orders from him and that after she put out his supper, she jolly well better lay out his evening clothes.

"I'm going out alone," he declared. "And you know who's going to dress me in my tuxedo and black tie?"

"Sure," said his wife, "the undertaker."

LATE ENTRY

The secretary came to work late. "Sorry, I had car trouble," she said to her boss.

"What happened?" he asked.

She, "I was a little late getting into it."

LATE IN LATE OUT

The salesman popped open one eye, glanced at his watch and groaned. His watch said 11 o'clock and he was supposed to be downstairs for the sales meeting at 9:30 A.M.

He grabbed the phone beside his bed and proceeded to chew out the desk clerk for failing to awaken him at 7:30 A.M. as requested. "Why," he demanded, "didn't your operator call me at 7:30?"

"Because," said the clerk, "you didn't come in to go to bed until 8:30 A.M."

LATE INCOME

The credit manager asked the wife applying for credit, "What is your husband's average income?"

"Usually around midnight!"

LATEST DOPE

The program chairman gave the sales speaker an overly flattering introduction, then said, "Now, we'll hear the latest dope from the American Association of Associates."

LAWFUL END

A defeated senator remarked to another ex-senator to be, "I dread the thought of returning home and trying to make ends meet under some of the laws I helped pass!"

LEAD STORY

City editors have always been on the look-out for a story about "Man Bites Dog." Now they look for the lead story "Bull Throws Salesman."

LEGAL ADVICE

"Who told you that you could loaf around the office without working, just because I kissed you a few times?" an annoyed boss asked his secretary.

"My attorney," she replied pertly.

LEGAL REMORSE

The widow had been to court eight times, had hired three different lawyers and a fourth to sue the first three, and still hadn't been able to wade through the legal red tape to collect her insurance money.

"With all this trouble," she finally shrieked one day, "there are times when I wish my husband hadn't died!"

LEMON WITHOUT A LEMON

An overly fussy sales manager gave his newly hired salesman a minute-by-minute schedule for his first sales trip.

7:00 A.M. Arrive at airport.

7:30 A.M. Take Eastern Flight 007.

8:45 A.M. At Cleveland terminal, have a cup of tea.

9:00 A.M. Take cab to customer's office.

Just before nine o'clock the sales manager received a wire from his neophyte salesman which read: "No lemon for tea in terminal restaurant. What do I do now?"

LETTER OPENER

The bright-eyed salesman bounced up the steps, rang the doorbell and was greeted by the man of the house.

"Good morning, sir," said the young man, cheerfully. "Want to buy a letter opener?"

"Buy one?" snorted the disgruntled husband. "I married one!"

LICENSE TO SELL

Policeman to door-to-door salesman: "You need a license to sell."

Salesman: "I knew I couldn't sell, but I didn't know that was the reason!"

LICENSES NOT WORKING

Many of the people who qualify for licenses to sell real estate don't work at it. And it could be said, with justification, that this includes those real estate salesmen who are continually sitting in their offices.

LIE DETECTION

"I'm Bob Henry, from Virginia," said the happy tobacco salesman to the Massachusetts store owner.

"O.K., glad to meet you," said the merchant. "And by the way, when you meet another Virginian, can you look at him and tell whether he's lying? We can up here."

"No, I can't," replied Bob. "Has it got something to do with watching whether his ears twitch or his eyes shift?"

"No," said the storekeeper, "It's much easier than that. If his lips are moving, we know he's lying. Now what was it you wanted to tell me?"

LIGHTED DULLNESS

Real estate agent: "What do you think of our snug community?"

Prospect: "It has to be the first cemetery I ever saw with lights!"

LIKE A SON

One sales manager said to a fired salesman, "In a way, though, I'll be sorry to lose you. You've been like a son to me—insolent, surly, and unappreciative!"

LIMITATIONS OF AUTOMATION

Automation won't replace the inept salesman. They still haven't invented a business machine that does absolutely nothing!

LIMITED ACQUAINTANCE

I know you well enough to borrow from you, but not well enough to lend to you.

LIMITED DEATH

Insurance agent to difficult prospect: "And how much insurance do you have?"

Difficult prospect: "About $10,000."

Insurance agent: "With that coverage, you don't expect to stay dead very long, do you?"

LIMITED PASSING

A college grid coach had just lost his out-standing freshman prospect by way of academic dismissal.

Sportswriter: "It sure is going to be quite a loss to the team!"

Sympathetic coach: "It sure is. Why that boy could do anything with a football except autograph it!"

LIMITED RETIREMENT

The salesman claimed he had enough money to last the rest of his life provided he died tomorrow morning.

LIVING CREDIT

The suit he bought was real cool. The wool was grown in Australia, the cloth was woven in New England, the thread comes from India, the suit was made in New York and he bought it on credit in Buenos Aires. It's remarkable that so many people can make a living out of things people haven't paid for.

LIVING ON THE CUFF

Many of us drive in a bank-financed car, on the bond-financed parkway, with gas charged to a credit-card, to open a charge account at a department store, so we can fill our savings-and-loan-financed home, with installment-purchased furniture.

LOADED BASEBALL FAN

"A salesman watched the Mets play the Yankees Wednesday night. In the top of the ninth, the bags were loaded and he was feeling no pain either!"

LOADED EARS

A purchasing agent was growing hard of hearing and went to the doctor. The doctor examined him and said, "I think you are drinking too much."

"How is that, Doc?" asked the purchasing agent, cupping his ear.

"You are drinking too much," shouted the doctor.

"Well, maybe I am," said the agent.

Six weeks later he came to see the doctor and he was hearing perfectly. Six weeks after that he was back in the doctor's office with almost no hearing at all.

"I thought when you stopped drinking you were hearing all right," said the doctor.

"I was Doc, but I liked what I was drinking so much better than what I was hearing that I went back to drinking again."

LOADED OBSERVATION

Two feminine characters at the ball park had been nipping steadily and finally finished the bottle. They then tossed the empty under the seat in front of them.

Just at that precise moment the fan in front of them, turned to his companion and said, "It's the bottom of the fifth and the bags are loaded!"

LOAN FOR THE FUTURE

A sales trainee noticed two women with the sales manager. Later in the day he asked, "Who were those two girls I saw you with?"

"One of them was my wife and the other was Liz Taylor," the sales manager explained.

"Which one was Liz Taylor?" asked the trainee.

The sales manager reached into his pocket, took out a dollar and handed it to the trainee.

"What's this for?" asked the trainee.

"Nothing," replied his boss. "I just want you to remember when you get to be president, that I once lent you money."

LOAN IN REVERSE

A farm hired hand walked into the bank of the small New England town and asked for a loan.

"Certainly," said the banker. "Just have your employer sign this note."

The hired hand was back the next day with a message scrawled on the back of the note by the farmer who employed him. The message, addressed to the banker, said: "You sign this note and I'll lend him the money!"

LOCKED OUT SALESMEN

The sales manager wasn't very considerate when he had his sales staff over to his house for a beer party—he locked the bathroom.

LOGICAL SITUATION

Three young women were attending the same logic class given at one of the better universities. During a lecture the professor stated that he was going to test their ability at situation reasoning.

"Let us assume," said the professor, "that you are aboard a small craft alone in the Pacific, and you spot a vessel approaching you with several thousand sex-starved sailors on board. What would you do in this situation to avoid any problem?"

"I would attempt to turn my craft in the opposite direction," stated the redhead.

"I would pass them trusting my knife to keep me safe," responded the brunette.

"Frankly," murmured the blonde, "I understand the situation, but I fail to see the problem."

LONG AND SHORT OF IT

If bank books aid a salesman's longevity, his wife's credit cards abet his shortevity!

LONG FORM—SHORT MEMORY

The applicant for a loan told the finance company interviewer, "Now that I have completed all of these forms, I've forgotten what I needed the loan for."

LONG TIME BETWEEN SALES

A salesman bragged that while selling he never drank, but then he couldn't remember whether it was '65 or '66 the last time he sold anything.

LOOSE PIN

The sales manager of a fast-growing outfit sticks pins in a big relief map behind his desk to show where every one of his salesmen is at a given moment. Burke, from the Chicago territory, was not, in the opinion of the manager, living up to his early promise, and was summoned to the home office for a pep talk and re-indoctrination.

"I'm not saying you're in imminent danger yet of being fired," was the stern finale of the sales manager's warning, "but if you'll look carefully at my map, Burke, you'll note I've loosened your pin!"

LOSS FOR WORDS

Prospect: "Make it snappy. I'm a man of few words."
Salesman: "Good, sign here. I'm selling dictionaries."

LOUD SUGGESTION

An employer had spent a great deal of money to ensure that his men should work under the best conditions.

"Now whenever I enter this workshop," he said, "I want to see every man cheerfully performing his task, and therefore I invite you to place in this box any further suggestions as to how that can be brought about."

A week later the box was opened; it contained only one slip of paper, on which was written: "Don't wear Hush-Puppies."

LOW AND SEXY

A cute Louisiana coed helped pay her tuition by landing a part-time job with a vacuum cleaner company. Hers was the task of demonstrating and taking orders on a new lightweight model, and she soon turned in sheafs of orders that doubled those of experienced salesmen on the staff.

"How do you do it?" marveled the manager in Baton Rouge.

"Nothing to it," she laughed. "I just address my sales talk to the husband in tones so low that his wife doesn't dare to miss a single word."

LOWER CONCENTRATION

In these days of low-cut gowns and mini-skirts, it takes concentration for a man to look a woman in the eye!

M

MACHINIST

An inept salesman filling out an employment application pondered a minute on the question: "What machines can you operate?"

Then he wrote: "Slot and pinball."

MAD LETTER

At a sales convention in a distant city, a salesman received a letter, which he opened, and quickly threw in a wastebasket.

"Who's it from?" asked a salesman friend.

"From my wife."

The other picked up the letter and looked at it. "But this is a blank page. There's nothing written on it."

"I know," said the first salesman. "My wife got mad when I told her I was coming to the convention without her. Now we're not speaking."

MADISON AVENUE DREAMS

A student at the Pace College of Business explained why he had chosen the field: "I have dreams of making a million dollars in advertising, just like my father."

The college dean asked, "When did your father make a million in advertising?"

"He didn't," said the student, "but he had dreams, too."

MAID OF EXPERIENCE

Hotel manager to newly hired maid: "Did you knock on the door of Room 614?"

New maid: "Yes, but he didn't answer, so I had to go in and wake him up."

Manager: "Don't you know better than to go into a traveling salesman's room?"

Maid: "I do now!"

MALE EFFICIENCY

My wife doesn't care how good looking my secretary is—just as long as *he* is efficient.

MANAGERIAL SAMPLING

Sales Manager: "Waiter, I want to order one of those lunches my salesmen charge on their expense accounts!"

MANLY DENOMINATOR

The thing that separates the men from the boys is the price of auto insurance!

MARITAL GOAL

The salesman was confiding to a fellow salesman that he had been aimlessly drifting, until he married. But now, after 30 years of marriage, he had a definite objective—revenge.

MARRIED TIP

In a night club you can always tell the difference between a single couple, an engaged couple, and a married couple. Just watch them when the check comes.

A single fellow picks up the check, leaves a tip, helps the young lady on with her coat, and off they go.

The engaged fellow picks up the check, she gives him the money, he leaves a tip, helps her on with her coat, and off they go.

A married fellow picks up the check, leaves a tip, she picks up half of it, puts on her own coat and off they go.

MATERNITY CLOTHES

A gal dialed the real estate office in error and in a soft feminine voice asked, "Do you sell maternity clothes?"

The salesman answered, "No, madam, but how about a larger house?"

MEANINGFUL EXPLANATION

A certain worker in the shipping department had been solicited several times by the Community Fund worker of his plant. They explained how his contribution would aid the aged and infirm, the destitute, and the city's other unfortunates. Their pattern of persuasion didn't work. He refused to give.

The situation was reported to the boss who called him and said flatly, "We're going to have 100% support for the fund in this plant. If you don't come through on this, Joe, you can look for another job.

"You mean that?" asked Joe.

"I sure do," was the reply.

"Here's my money," said Joe, "I think it's a fine cause. I would have given before, but this is the first time it's been explained to me."

MECHANICAL GOOFING

There's a new office machine that takes the place of three gals:
   (a) Goes to washroom 26 times.
   (b) Makes 48 personal phone calls.
   (c) Takes 5 coffee breaks.
   (d) Takes up a collection every other pay day.

MEDICAL COVER-UP

Inept executive, after a physical examination: "Doctor, level with me. If there's anything wrong, give it to me in plain English—no medical language."

Doctor: "I'll level with you. You're just plain lazy and need more exercise."

Inept executive: "In that case, give me the medical term, so I can tell my boss."

MEETINGITIS

Sales manager's secretary: "Mr. Wilson can't take your order now. He's in a sales meeting."

MEMORABLE EVENINGS

The sales manager's secretary was asked, "What has been the most memorable day for you at the office?"

The secretary thought for a minute, then answered, "I don't remember the day but I do remember the night."

MINI-EFFORT

A businessman explained why he fired his secretary for wearing miniskirts: "She was still able to do an excellent job, but I wasn't!"

MINI ROMANCE

They stood at the door. Her attitude was firm. He was pleading.
He: "If I might . . ."
She: "No."
He: "But . . ."
She: "I don't wish to hear . . ."
He: "One word?"
She: "Not one."
And then she shut the door and the door-to-door salesman went on to the next call.

MINI SCREWDRIVER

For a half hour, the head of the house worked to get the sagging door to swing straight.

"Hey son," he called to his boy, "get me a big screwdriver, will you please?"

After a long time—it seemed like hours—the boy returned empty handed.

Apologetically he said, "Gee Dad, I've got the orange juice, but I can't find enough vodka in the house for even a little screwdriver."

MINIMIZE THE DISTRACTIONS

"Tell me, Hank," a friend asked a young businessman, "how do you expect to accomplish anything at your office with three good-looking stenographers around?"

"Easy," said Hank. "I'll give two of them the same day off!"

MINIMUM WAGES

Boss to stockroom clerk: "I'd like to pay you what you're worth, but I don't want to break the minimum wage law!"

MISSED OPPORTUNITIES

Sales Manager: "Honey, what did you think of my speech?"

Sales manager's wife: "Earl, it seemed to me you didn't take advantage of all of your opportunities."

Sales manager: "How do you mean?"

Wife: "You passed up several opportunities to sit down before you did."

MISSING MAILING ADDRESS

The inept salesman was seen rushing out of an office building, going to his car, searching the inside, then turning the trunk inside out.

A passing policeman inquired, "What are you looking for?"

The inept salesman replied, "I've just been handed a sales order and I can't find the address of my company!"

MISTAKES FOR SALE

It's a shame that mistakes can't be sold for as much as they cost!

MISUNDERSTOOD HONEY

A salesman taking his wife on one of his selling trips ordered pancakes for breakfast at one of the hotels where he generally spent the night.

When the waitress brought the pancakes he asked, "Where's my honey?"

The waitress replied, "Oh she left last week for another job."

MODEL HOMES

The real estate salesman spent all day Sunday showing a couple through model homes.

"And here," he said wearily at the tenth home he had shown, "is the hobby room. Do you folks have any hobbies?"

"Yes," replied the woman, "looking through model homes on Sunday!"

MODEST KNOCK

Just after a salesman was admitted to the hospital, he heard a knock at the door of his room. "Come in," he said. And in came a woman.

"I'm your doctor," she said. "Please take off your clothes."

He asked her if she meant for him to remove all of his clothing, and she told him that was just what she did mean. So he took off all of his clothes and she examined him.

When she finished her examination, she announced: "You may get into bed. Now do you have any questions?" "Just one," he said. "Why did you knock?"

MOM'S THE CHAMP

A young bully stuck his finger in a timid boy's face and said, "Listen you, my father can lick your father!"

Timid, but bright boy, "Big deal. So can my mother!"

MONEY BACK?

A real estate salesman had just closed his first deal, only to discover the lot he had sold was under water.

"My customer's going to come back here mighty mad," he complained to the boss. "Shall I give him his money back?"

"Money back!" roared the boss, "What kind of a salesman are you? Get out there and sell him a motorboat!"

MONEY NO GOOD

A salesman in a new territory was warned not to call on a particular dealer.

"Why?" asked the salesman.

"His credit is so bad even his money isn't accepted," was the answer.

MORNING AFTER

The salesman refused to tell the guys in the office how his first honeymoon night went. But, he did comment that when they came to the dining room for breakfast, they both asked for separate checks.

MORNING BLUES

"Tell me, Mr. Rapport," said the marriage counselor, after several sessions, "did you wake up grouchy this morning?"

"No," said Rapport, "I let her sleep. Besides I'm tired of getting up every morning with a nagging headache—her!"

MORNING ECONOMY

Summoned to the accounting office, the salesman was confronted by the comptroller, "This expense account amazes us. How do you manage to spend $14.00 a day for food for yourself?"

The salesman replied, "I manage, by skipping breakfast!"

MOTIVATING WIFE

A man who had become very wealthy through his own efforts was asked by a friend how it all happened.

"A lot of credit goes to my wife," the millionaire informed him.

"How did she help you?" the friend asked.

"Well, to be perfectly frank," the wealthy man replied, "I was curious to see if there was any income beyond which she couldn't live."

MRS. CUTIE PIE

Accompanied by his wife, the good-looking salesman got on the elevator. On the way down, an amply endowed young secretary got on board and greeted the salesman with, "Hi there, cutie pie."

Without batting an eye, his wife turned to the secretary and said, "And I'm Mrs. Pie."

MULTIPLED WRINKLES

A fellow shopping at a bargain store admired a pair of pants and asked if they'd hold a crease.

"Hold a crease!" exclaimed the salesman. "They'd hold a million of them!"

MURDER AT THE EXCHANGE

The best way to make a killing in the stock market is to shoot your broker!

MUTUAL ILLNESS

"What exactly do you mean when you say you left your last sales job because of illness?"

"Well, it was kind of mutual illness, I got sick of them and they got sick of me!"

MY ACHING BACK

A shoe salesman who had gone back and forth from the stock room to the fitting room, trying on dozens of pairs of shoes on a fussy lady, finally asked her, "May I please pause for a few minutes? Your feet are breaking my back!"

MY THREE SONS

A mother was discussing her three sons with a new acquaintance.

Mother: "My Robert is a dentist and William is an attorney."

New friend: "You must be proud of them. What does your other son do?"

Mother: "He's a salesman and supports Bob and Bill."

N

NAGGING EXPERT

A wife told a newly met friend: "My husband is an efficiency expert."

New friend: "What does an efficiency expert do?"

Wife: "Well, if we women did it, they'd call it nagging."

NAME THE DREAM

Two wives were complaining about their husbands.

One said, "My husband sometimes stays out all night and, when he does get home, he hardly speaks to me."

"That's nothing," the other said, "when my husband comes home from a business trip, he pays no attention to me until the middle of the night. Then he strokes me gently and murmurs, 'Come on honey, tell me your real name.' "

NAMELESS PROBLEM

"Man, am I scared," a friend confided to his pal at the bar. "I just got a card from a guy saying that he'd shoot me if I didn't stay away from his wife."

"Well, stay away from his wife and you've got no problem," advised his pal.

"How can I?" he lamented. "He didn't sign his name."

NATIONALITY INDICATOR

The men who run international automobile shows have developed an interesting philosophy determining the nationality of show visitors. If a visitor opens the hood and looks at the engine, he is German.

If he is interested in the style and lines of the car, he is French.

If he tries the horn, he is Italian.

And if he checks the size and price tag, he is American.

NEGATIVE ADVERTISING

Headline of bank ad offering premiums for new depositors: "For all you no-accounts!"

NEIGHBORLY ITEM

Door-to-door salesman: "I'd like to show you a little item your neighbors told me you couldn't afford!"

NEIGHBORLY LEAD

Mrs Jones, to a door-to-door appliance salesman, "No, I don't want a new portable sewing machine but, please go next door. I always borrow her machine and it's about time she got a new one."

NEIGHBORLY MOTIVE

Auto dealer: "Ralph, I think this is the right time to sell the Allens a car.

Auto salesman: "Why do you think so?"

Auto dealer: "Their next door neighbor just bought a new car."

NEIGHBOR'S GREEN

"I can't make them out," said the village gossip over the back fence. "They have no car, no piano, no television, and she hasn't any jewelry and no furs."

"Probably," said her neighbor, "they just have no money."

NEOPHYTE VICTIM

A hold-up man demanded money from the bank's newest teller. "Don't bother me," she said, "I'm just a beginner!"

NERVOUS MEETING ATTENDEE

At one of our sales meetings a fellow flinched every time an automobile horn was sounded on the street. He disturbed the others so much, the meeting was stopped and he was asked why he was acting this way.

He answered, "A few days ago, my wife ran away with a cab driver and every time I hear an auto horn, I'm afraid it's the cab driver, bringing her back!"

NEVER ON MONDAY

It was love at first sight for the jewelry salesman and the department store buyer. One month later they were married and they left on a Friday for a week-end honeymoon in the Poconos.

It was a rapturous three days for both of them. But on Monday morning the bride had departed with no explanatory note.

The groom returned immediately to their home city and was unable to find out her whereabouts. Heartbroken, he returned to his office and told his sales manager what had happened.

The sales manager told him, "I'm surprised at you getting all upset. You should know that she never sees salesmen on Mondays!"

NEW FIRE POLICY

One insurance salesman said to another, "We have a new fire policy at our office."

"What is it?" he was asked.

"If I don't sell this policy, I'll get fired!" was the reply.

NEW MATH

The dean wouldn't allow the star football player to play in the big game coming up on Saturday. The coach brought the player into the dean's office and cried, "Why don't you let him play Saturday? We need him!"

"I'll tell you why," shot back the dean. "This is supposed to be a school of learning. All he knows is football, and I'll show you how ignorant he is!"

Then he said to the player, "Tell me, how much is two and two?"

"Seven," came the answer.

With that, the coach cried to the dean, "Aw, let him play. After all, he only missed by one!"

NEWS–GOOD AND BAD

A salesman, returning home from work, said to his wife, "The good news is I'm in the vanguard of the fight against inflation. The bad news is I'm fired!"

NEWSWORTHY

The headline in a newspaper read: "COMPANY CANS 500 MEN."

To which the old maid responded, "Oh boy, I've been waiting a long time for this product to be packaged!"

99 44/100% PERFECT

The closest most of us ever get to perfection is when we fill out an employment application.

NO-ACCOUNT CUSTOMER

A new sales clerk asked the customer, "Do you have an account here, Madam?"

The customer replied, "No, please show me where the manager is."

The new sales clerk led her to the manager's office and said, "A no-account lady to see you, boss."

NO-HITTER

Staggering and groggy, the prize fighter stumbled back to his corner. He had taken a terrific one-sided beating for six rounds.

"Don't give up now, boy," his manager whispered in his ear. "You've got a no-hitter going!"

NO ORDER TAKER

An inept salesman angrily told his sales manager, "Don't talk to me that way! I'm not accustomed to taking orders from anyone."

The sales manager retorted, "That's exactly what I'm talking about. You definitely are not accustomed to taking orders—of any kind!"

NO VACANCY

After the inept salesman was fired, no effort was made to hire any one else to take his place. He had left no vacancy!

NOBODY BUT NOBODY

Inept salesman: "I don't suppose you don't know of nobody who don't want to hire nobody to do nothing don't you?"
Sales manager: "Yes, I don't!"

NON-SUPPER

After three days at a convention in the Catskills, tipping doormen, bellboys, waitresses and bartenders, the salesman got so fed up that he wouldn't even answer the door.

But one evening there was a persistent knock on his door and he responded, "Who is it?"

"Telegram for you," the bellboy replied.

"Slip it under the door, please."

"I'm sorry sir," the bellboy answered, "I can't."

"Why can't you?" he was asked.

"Because the telegram is on a tray."

NON-TRAVELING SALESMAN

A candidate for a selling job was asked on an application: "How many miles are there in a round trip from Boston to Los Angeles?"

He told the interviewer, "If that's going to be my territory, I don't want the job."

NOTHING FOR MANAGEMENT

The industrial tycoon, having trouble with sleeping, visited his doctor. The doctor tried to soothe his nerves by talking, but failed to help him sleep. Next the doctor prescribed a mild sedative, but it did not do any good. A strong sedative was tried, but this, too, produced no sleep. Finally, the physican wrote out a prescription for a pill strong enough to knock out a horse.

When the pill brought no relief, the tycoon told the doctor, "My wife had some women in last night. They were talking about twilight sleep. Would that help me, Doc?"

"No," said the physican, "twilight sleep is only for labor."

The tycoon banged his fist down, "That's the trouble with this country," he exploded. "Never have anything for management!"

OBVIOUS SUSPECT

There was a big break-in at the local drug store the other night. Everything was taken out of the store that night, excepting birth-control pills and hair tonics. The police are looking for a bald-headed Catholic!

OFF DAY FIRING

The eager beaver box boy at the supermarket was going home on a Tuesday night when the boss suddenly told him he was fired.

"Fired?" he yelled. "But, Mr. Hansen, I've worked like a slave all day long. I've swept the floors, arranged the stock, waited on customers."

"Maybe you did," conceded Mr. Hansen, "but you didn't empty the garbage, clean the windows or hose down the sidewalk."

"But Mr. Hansen," the boy screamed, "This is my day off!"

OFFICE TEAMWORK

Every office needs an executive to dream up an idea; an assistant to point why it can't be done and a secretary to do it!

OLD FAITHFUL

After the sales meeting, during the "happy hour," one traveling salesman said to the other salesman, "I understand you're going out to the West Coast on your next trip."

"And I'm certainly going to take in the sights on that trip!"

"Be sure you see Old Faithful."

"See it? I'm taking her with me!"

100 PROOF QUALITY

"My husband is the silliest guy," one bridge player told another.

"What's he done now?" the other asked.

"I went to the service station with him this morning, and he asked the station attendant a thousand questions about the make and manufacturer before he let him put oil into the car. But when he went into a bar, he poured down the stuff and never asked the bartender a single question!"

ONE STOP DESTITUTION

The way inflation is running now, old folks can file for social security and bankruptcy at the same time!

1000 LIKE YOU

A salesman presented a new line to a prospect, but the prospect insisted on thinking it over.

"That's okay, sir, I wish I had a hundred like you," said the salesman.

A week later he was back, gave the same excellent pitch and got the same response; the guy insisted on thinking it over. Again the salesman's comment was, "That's okay, sir, I wish I had a hundred like you."

This went on and on until finally the prospect couldn't stand it and said to the salesman, "You've been calling on me for seven months, I've never given you a dime, yet you always smile and say 'I wish I had a hundred like you.' Why?"

The salesman's answer, "Because, man, I've got a thousand like you."

ON TIME ORDERLINESS

Two foremen were comparing notes.

"Do all the boys in your shop drop their tools the moment the whistle blows?" asked one.

"No, not at all," replied the other. "The orderly ones have their tools put away long before that time."

ORDER FIRST!

Prospect: "Get out of here before I throw you out."

Salesman: "Go ahead! I don't mind as long as you give me the order first."

ORDERS TAKE PRECEDENCE

When a cold-hearted sales manager heard that one of his salesman had been found dead in Philadelphia, he sent this wire to the police: "Send samples back by parcel post and search the body for orders."

"OR ELSE!"

The salesman rushed into the sales manager's office and demanded, "I want a bigger rate of commission or else!"

"Or else, what?" the manager asked in disdain.

"Or else I'll go back and sell for the commissions I'm now getting."

OUT-DATED JOKE

The traveling salesman asked the farmer to put him up for the night.

Farmer: "Sure, but you'll have to sleep with my son."

Salesman: "Oh no, I'm in the wrong joke."

OUT OF SIGHT

"I know I'm not much to look at," admitted the salesman who had just proposed.

"Oh well," philosophized his bride to be, "You'll be on the road most of the time!"

OUT-TALKED

After a long introduction, the speaker opened his talk by saying, "I'm in the position of the man who said 'Last night my wife and I had words, but I didn't get a chance to use mine!' "

OVER-COMPENSATION

If you are one of those critics who think we are getting too much government, just imagine for a minute what it would be like if we were ever to get as much as we are paying for.

OVER-COOKED SPEECH

An executive with a deep coat of tan was asked by one of his fellow executives, "Did you get your tan playing golf?"

The executive replied, "No, I spoke at an out-door sales meeting in Miami."

The fellow executive remarked, "If you got that brown, you definitely talked too long."

OVER PAID ORDER-TAKERS

Some inept salesmen are little more than overpaid stock clerks carrying an attache case and an order pad. They even have trouble giving away free samples!

OVER SELLING

Catholic mother to daughter, madly in love with a Jewish boy:
"Sell him the idea of the beauty and joy of being a Catholic."
The daughter did and she sold him.
Mother: "Good! Don't stop selling him!
One day before the marriage, the daughter came home in tears.
Daughter: "It's off!"
Mother: "Why? Didn't you sell him?"
Daughter: "I oversold him! Now he wants to be a priest!"

OVER-TRAINED

Executive: "How is it you never come to work on time anymore?"
Secretary: "Well boss, it's like this; you've done such a good job of educating me not to be a clock-watcher during office hours that I've lost the habit of watching it at home."

P

PAID FEATURE

A customer, after listening to an auto salesman tell him about the new features of this year's model, floored the salesman when he said, "My three year old car has one feature that is unmatched by new models—it's paid for."

PAID IN FULL DRIVING

A finance company representative had to remind a kindly old farmer that he hadn't paid the last two of 50 installments on a new car.

"It's in the barn," said the farmer sadly, and in a low voice, so his wife couldn't hear, "Sickness cost us too much this year. I'm afraid you'll have to take that car of yours back."

The representative reluctantly walked to the barn. There he was amazed to find the automobile shiny and new, up on blocks, carefully covered with a tarpaulin, with the meter showing only 12 miles—the distance from the auto salesroom to the farmer's barn.

"But you've never driven this car!" exclaimed the representative.

"Didn't feel I should," nodded the farmer. "I figured she's not mine 'till she's fully paid for."

PAINFUL CLIMB

It was the executive's first visit and he determinedly gave the doctor a long, dull case history. Finally he concluded, "After the first, I'm tired, Doc. After the second, my chest aches and I start getting pains in my legs. After the third, I feel like fainting and it takes a half-hour for my pulse and respiration to return to normal."

"Then why don't you quit after the first?" asked the doctor.

"How can I?" came the answer. "I live on the third floor!"

PAINFUL OPINION

Two salesmen were talking about their district sales manager. One said, "To me, he's a pain in the neck!"

The other salesman replied, "That's funny, I have a much lower opinion of him!"

PAR FOR THE KITCHEN

First executive: "I'd rather play golf than eat."

Second executive: "But doesn't your wife object?"

First executive: "No, she'd rather play bridge than cook."

PARTIAL SALES FORCE

"How many salesmen work for you?"

The sales manager answered. "Just about half!"

PARTING IS SUCH SWEET SORROW

Word had gotten around to the sales manager that his salesmen were taking his secretary out after hours.

He confronted his salesmen at the Monday morning meeting and asked, "How many of you guys have been dating my secretary?"

All but one admitted that they had been unable to resist the temptation to take her out. The sales manager then turned to the one salesman who had not dated the secretary and said to him, "You're the guy we're looking for. Go out and tell her she's fired!"

PARTNERS

Stockroom clerk: "Isn't this beautiful weather we are having?"
Boss: "We? All of a sudden you're a partner!"

PARTY BUILDERS—BANQUET WRECKERS

Lately there appears to be a convention for everything. Look upon the events bulletin board of any large hotel and you'll usually see a long list of meetings.

Sometimes the list can pull you up short, as did this actual notice in the Park Plaza Motel in Toronto:

Metro Home Builders . . . Cocktail Party
Metro House Wreckers Assn . . . Banquet

PASSING MILES

A star athelete had flunked a geography course, then agreed to take an oral test.

"Answer one question," the teacher said, "and I'll pass you. What is the capital of New Jersey?"

"Princeton," the boy replied.

"You're wrong," the teacher roared. "That's all for you."

The boy's coach protested. "The capital is Trenton, which is 12 miles from Princeton. And 12 from 100 leaves 88, and 88 is passing in any school."

PASSION LIMIT

A doctor warned a sales executive who was a heart attack victim, not to smoke, drink or dance during his convalescence.

"What about kissing?" asked the patient.

The medic answered, "Only with your wife. I don't want you to get excited."

PATIENT INVESTOR

The only thing I've learned about the stock market is that you have to be patient. And the way it's been going lately, I'm going to become one!

PAUSE THAT REFRESHES

The prospect stated to the salesman who had just paused after a lengthy sales talk, "You know I just noticed something remarkable about your presentation."

The salesman inquired, "What is it?"

The prospect answered, "The pause you just took."

PAYMENT DURABILITY

How long does an appliance last? Two minutes longer than the final payment!

PAYS FOR ITSELF

A lady walked into an appliance store and asked to see some toasters. A high pressure salesman decided instead to sell her an expensive freezer.

"Madame," he pitched. "Believe me when I tell you that this freezer will pay for itself in no time at all."

"Fine," said the lady. "As soon as it does send it over."

PENTAGON EFFICIENCY

After careful investigation, the new clerk found thousands and thousands of old documents in his files, none of which served any purpose whatsoever. He promptly applied to the head of the department for permission to burn them.

After two months, back came the answer: "Yes, but be careful to make copies of the documents first, and see that the copies are carefully filed."

PERMISSIVENESS

A woman bought a $250 suit at an exclusive shop and was appalled to see what appeared to be the same suit on the rack of a department store for $59.95.

She rushed back to the swank shop to complain.

"But, Madam," said the saleslady, "the copy you saw in the department store wasn't 100% virgin wool!"

"At these prices I should care what the sheep do at night!" the woman replied.

PERSISTENT ORDER-TAKER

A salesman came into a busy lawyer's office and asked, "How about buying some ties?"

"Get out of here. I don't need any," the lawyer said, brushing him off.

"They're the latest designs."

"Didn't you hear what I just told you?"

"Look at the width and length of these ties."

At that moment the attorney got up and bodily threw the salesman out with his box of ties.

The salesman got up from the lobby floor and picked up his scattered supply of ties, walked back into the prospect's office and said, "Now that you've had your fun, I'm ready to take your order."

PERSUASIBLE SALE

A young salesman, forever boasting of his selling persuasiveness, was told by his sales manager, "I'm amazed at you. You brag of being our top salesman, yet you haven't persuaded me into increasing your salary!"

PICTURE SALESMAN

Businessman: "What do you do with all those pictures you paint?"

Artist: "I sell them."

Businessman: "Name your terms, man, I've been looking for a salesman like you for years."

"PLAY BALL!"

An innocent young stenographer after her first day on the job, went shopping in a sporting goods store. She ordered all the equipment necessary for a baseball game, including a baseball, a bat, a catcher's mitt and a catcher's mask.

"Are you sure you want all of these?" asked the salesman.

The young stenographer answered, "Yes, I do, my boss said that if I'd play ball with him, we'd get along fine!"

POINT OF NO RETURN

A well known sales speaker was admitting to a fellow speaker that he was losing confidence in his ability to speak. He asked his colleague, "Did you ever get that feeling?"

The colleague replied, "Yes, once after I had been speaking for twelve years, it suddenly occurred to me that I had very limited talents for platform speaking."

"What did you do?"

"What could I do? By then, I already had a renowned reputation as a sales speaker."

POINTS TO COME BACK

"Good news! I've just earned enough points for us to go to Europe on the company's incentive contest," shouted the salesman to his wife.

"Wonderful!" shrieked his wife, "when do we leave?"

"As soon as I've earned enough points for us to come back," he explained.

POLITICAL AGILITY

It was said of a prominent politician: "He's more agile now than when he was a baby. At least, he's putting his foot in his mouth more now!"

POLLUTION SOLUTION

The political candidates can take the first big step toward ending our air pollution problems—they should stop making speeches!

POP AGREES

Two young boys were talking.

"My father is better than your father!"

"No, he's not!"

"My brother is better than your brother!"

"No, he's not."

"My mother is better than your mother!"

"Well, I guess you've got me there. My father says the same thing."

POPULARITY IN REVERSE

Salesman: "I'll have to have a raise, there are three other companies after me."

Sales manager: "Is that so? What companies?"

Salesman: "Light, phone and gas!"

POPULATION EXPLOSION

A current survey on the population explosion discloses that there are three reasons for the high birth rate--early marriages, drive-in movies, and rock festivals.

POSITIVE ACTION

One salesman has finally stopped arguing with his 16-year-old son about borrowing the car. Now, whenever the salesman wants the car, he takes it!

POSITIVE CALLS

Three umpires were discussing problems of their profession.

The first said, "Some's balls and some's strikes, and I call's 'em as they is."

The second said, "Some's balls and some's strikes, and I calls 'em as I sees 'em."

The third said, "I sees 'em comin' across and some's balls and some's strikes, but they ain't nothin' 'til I calls 'em."

POSITIVE NAGGING

A certain salesman started to storm out of the house after an argument with his wife.

"You'll be back," she screamed at him. "How long do you think you'll be able to stand 'happiness'?"

POSITIVE THINKING

A depressed new salesman was looking for counsel from a salesman who has been traveling and selling for the past 30 years.

Older salesman: "What's your problem?"

Younger salesman: "It seems that on every call I make, I get insulted!"

Older salesman: "I can't understand your getting that kind of treatment. I've been pushed out of the door into the street, I've had my briefcase thrown at me, I've been called a low sneaking, conniving scoundrel, but *never insulted!*"

POSSESSIVE EXCUSE

An auto dealer asked the inept salesman who had just escorted a customer through the showroom door, "How come he didn't buy?"

"Oh, I didn't try to sell him," the salesman replied, "after I found out he already owned a car."

POWERIZED

I bought one of those foreign cars with power brakes, power steering, power seats, power ash trays—everything power. You don't drive it. You just sit there and tremble.

POWERLESS SALESMAN

A house-to-house salesman rang the bell of a little house on the outskirts of town. When the woman of the house opened the door, he tossed in on her living-room rug about a half-peck of unsavory looking road dust and sand.

"Now, Madam," he said, "don't get excited. This is just my way of demonstrating our Super-Duper vacuum cleaner. If the cleaner doesn't clean up that rug as slick as a whistle, I'll eat the rug!"

"Well," said the woman, "you better start eating. This is an all gas house."

PRACTICED HOOK

Florida tells the one about the two elderly ladies who, once every week, joined each other on the golf links.

On this particular day, one of the gals strode to the first tee, pulled back her club, closed her eyes and swung with all her might. The ball hooked off to the side, ricocheted off several trees and took a fantastic bounce onto the green and into the cup for a hole-in-one.

Her companion turned and frowned. "Betty, you sneak," she said icily, "you've been practicing!"

PREFERRED NOTHING

An unsuccessful businessman told one of his creditors, "I'm going into bankruptcy, but I'm making you a preferred creditor."

"What's that?" the creditor asked.

The businessman replied, "I'm telling you now that you're not going to collect a dime. The others won't know for 90 days!"

PREGNANT ACCOUNT

Memo from credit department: "Your account has been on our books for over a year and we would like to remind you that we have now carried you longer than your mother did."

PREGNANT QUESTION

It had been a hectic day for the new sales girl in the maternity department of the discount store. The store had been crowded with no let-up in customers from the time the doors opened. Just as she looked forward for a break, in came a new batch of expectant mothers.

She cried out, "Doesn't anyone do it for fun anymore?"

PRESENTATION THAT BOOMERANGED

Friend: "Driving a brand new car! Business must be good!"

Insurance man: "Not exactly, I made the mistake of trying to sell an insurance policy to the best automobile salesman I ever met!"

PRESSURING THE PRESSURER

My husband and I had been plagued beyond endurance by door-to-door salesmen, so when the "last straw" landed on our doorstep with a home improvement scheme, we turned the tables on him.

He had barely made the purpose of his mission known when we began our own sales pitch. We tried to sell him our car, our furniture, and anything else in sight.

He left in confusion, stammering apologies, for not making a purchase, and we collapsed, howling, on the couch.

Two days later, we were astonished to see him return. This time with a companion.

"I hope you folks won't mind," he said in his apologetic tone, "I brought my manager to meet you. He just wouldn't believe me!"

PRICED PICKING

Customer at vegetable counter: "What's the price of these tomatoes?"

Clerk: "Twenty-five cents a pound if we pick them out, fifty-cents a pound if you pick them up!"

PRICE NO OBJECT

Who cares how much anything costs as long as we don't pay now, but later—much later!

PRICE OF BANKRUPTCY

Prospect to salesman: "$220, ridiculous! I never paid your competitor over $160 in all the time I did business with him and that was right up to Thursday, the day they went into bankruptcy."

PRICE TAG FOR THE HUSBAND

Saleswoman in hat shop: "It's only $19.95, madam, and includes a $9.95 sales slip to show your husband.

PRICING VERSATILITY

A gentleman in the optical business was instructing his son in the technique of chiselling a fair and honest price out of a customer.

He said, "Son, after you have fitted the glasses to a customer, and the customer asks, 'What's the charge?' you should say: 'The charge is ten dollars.' Then pause and watch for the flinch. If the customer doesn't flinch, you say: 'That's for the frames, the lenses will be another ten dollars.' Then you pause again, but this time just slightly, and again you watch for the flinch. If the customer doesn't flinch, you say, 'Each.' "

PRIVATE PARKING

A prospective customer walked into a New York city auto showroom and told the floor salesman, "I want to buy that model in the window."

The auto salesman replied, "Good. It's priced at a modest $6,000. Do you want it delivered or would you prefer to drive it out?"

"No, just leave it in the window." the customer said, "I'll never get such a good parking space again."

PROBLEM SOLVER

A young beauty came to the psychiatrist's office. He dismissed his nurse, locked the door, then instructed the beautiful patient to embrace him. After a long passionate kiss, the psychiatrist said, "Well that solves my problem, now what's yours?"

PROCESS THE SOLUTION

The vice-president of one of our local banks objected to investing in a data processing machine, considering it a needless expense. The board of directors out-voted him, however, and plans for installation began. When delivery day came, it was discovered that the components were far too large to fit into the bank's elevator.

"How am I going to get this thing up to the third floor?" the delivery man moaned.

The vice-president saw no problem. "Plug it in," he said, "and let it figure it out for itself."

PROFESSIONAL PREFERENCE

One day, a salesman played a round of golf with the club pro. At the nineteenth hole, the salesman said, "Julius, what do you think of my game?"

Julius shrugged and replied, "Oh, I suppose it's all right, but I still prefer golf!"

PROMISE NOT TO PROMISE

A multi-millionaire who had made his way up in the business world, from a childhood of poverty, was on his deathbed and passing on some last minute advice to his only son.

"My boy," he said, "I owe my success to two principles; honesty and wisdom. Honesty is: if you promise to deliver an item, no matter what happens, even if it means bankruptcy, deliver!"

"I'll try to remember that, Dad," replied the boy. "And what about wisdom?"

"Wisdom is simple," answered his father: "just don't make any promises!"

PRONE DEBTOR

A credit manager received this letter: "I'm sorry I have not paid my account, but, you see, I just got married and I've been on my honeymoon. As soon as I get back on my feet again, I'll be sure to take care of it."

PROOF OF NEED

The following inter-office memo was sent to the sales department: "All salesmen wishing to take advantage of the stenographers in the pool must report to Miss Abbott and show evidence of their need."

PROPER FORM

The sales manager spent five weeks selecting and hiring the right secretary for himself. He knows it pays to have a good head on your shoulder and a good shape on your lap.

PROSPECTIVE SALESMAN

The appliance salesman had not been successful in selling a man and his wife a new dishwasher. However, the man still seemed to have an interest in the new dishwasher, because he asked the salesman, "Will you give me a commission if I sell one for you?"

"Of course, I'll give you $20," the appliance salesman replied.

The man proposed, "Let me show you how I sell one to my wife!"

PROTECTIVE ATTENDANCE

The problem in being a member of an executive's club is that you have to attend all the meetings in order to protect yourself from being put on a committee.

PUBLIC ISSUE

A financial executive came home unexpectedly and found his wife being embraced by a stranger. He yelled, "What is the meaning of this?"

His wife looked over to him and said, "Oh, haven't you heard? I've gone public."

PUGNACIOUS RELIEVER

The baseball manager was holding a skull session with a group of rookies in spring training.

"Just visualize this," he said to a young pitcher. "We're winning, 1 to 0, with the Mets at bat, in the last of the ninth. They have the bases loaded. Nobody out.

"At this point, you're called in as a relief pitcher to face Willie Mays. The count on him is three balls and no strikes. What would you do to get out of that hole?"

The kid scratched his head in deep thought for a moment. "Only thing I can see to do in a spot like that," he said, "is to pick a fight with the umpire and get kicked out of the game."

PUZZLED EXIT

The salesman's wife had left him so many times that last week she stood at the front door trying to remember if she was coming or going.

Q

QUALIFIED POSTMASTER

An ignorant precinct worker announced to his ward boss that in reward for his doorbell pulling activities for the party, he wanted to be made postmaster of his town.

"No, that kind of job isn't for you," said the boss. "Why you can't read or write."

"I don't want to be assistant postmaster," the guy replied. "I want to be postmaster!"

QUALIFYING DOORS

Things were getting the best of a salesman. So he made up his mind to visit a psychiatrist. There was only one in town, so he entered the door and found a room without a receptionist, just two other doors. One door was labeled "Men" and the other "Women."

He pushed open the door marked "Men" and was confronted by two more doors. One said, "Introverts," and the other "Extroverts." After a moment's hesitation he walked through the "Extroverts" door and found himself in still another room with two doors. These were carefully lettered: "You make less than $10,000 a year," and the other, "You make over $10,000 a year." There was no question where he belonged and he rushed through the under-$10,000 door and found himself right back on the street.

QUALIFYING THE DEAL

Real estate salesman to young couple: "How irresponsible are you two and how deep in debt are you willing to go?"

QUELLED IDEAS

Customer: "Do you have any notions on this floor?"

Floorwalker: "Oh yes, madam, but we try to suppress them during working hours."

QUESTION OF ETHICS

A partner defines business ethics: "For instance, I discover I've been given a $100 bill by mistake. Now comes the question of ethics. Should I, or should I not, tell my partner!"

QUESTION OF QUALITY

Male customer: "I want three pairs of nylon hose."
Saleslady: "Are these for your wife or do you want something better?"

QUESTIONABLE BRILLIANCE

Remember, just because nobody disagrees with you does not necessarily mean that you are brilliant. Maybe you're the boss.

QUESTIONED ABSENCE

Executive, referring to secretary missing for two days: "I don't know whether she's quit or is on a coffee break."

QUICK DECISION

Wife to salesman: "What are you getting me for my birthday, dear—a mink stole or a little sports car? But don't waste any time deciding—either one will make me very happy!"

QUICK HENRY, THE LISTERINE!

A staff of twenty-five salesmen left their sales office last week. Six resigned and the others told the sales manager about his breath.

QUIET HORN

New car buyer to service manager: "The only thing that doesn't make a noise in my car is the horn!"

QUOTE ACCEPTED

Customer: "What are you asking for that suit in the window?"
Salesman: "I'm not going to say $100, $90, $85—with me it's one price, $80."

Customer: "Isn't that funny. I'm exactly of the same nature—I'm not going to say $75, $70, or $65. By me, it's one price also, $50."

Salesman: "Sold!"

R

RAISING ONLY SEVEN

One salesman who's always late for sales meetings, tells his sales manager that there are eight in his family and his alarm clock was set for only seven.

RATTLING HEAD

I told the salesman that sold me my new car that I kept hearing this rattle, but he said it was all in my head.

REASSURANCE

If you're ever down and depressed, get out your copy of the last resume you wrote to apply for a job, and you'll realize what an admirable person you are!

RE-BUILT WIFE?

The farmer's barn had burned down and the agent from the insurance company arrived to discuss the claim. He explained the policy coverage on the structure, and told the farmer that the company would rather build another barn of similar size and materials, instead of paying the claim in cash.

The farmer was furious. "If that's the way your company does business," he exploded, "you can just cancel the insurance policy on my wife!"

RED TRUCK ON SCHEDULE

A husband and his wife were on an incentive trip that he had earned by doubling his sales quota. For his wife it was her first plane flight. The plane touched down in St. Louis on its way o the East Coast and a little red truck sped out to its side to refuel it.

The plane landed again at Cleveland and again the little red truck dashed out to its side. When the plane touched down at New York, again the little red truck sped up to the plane.

"This plane," said the husband, "sure makes wonderful time!"

"Yes," said the wife, "and that little red truck isn't doing bad either!"

REFERENCES

Sales manager: "Your references, please?"

Applicant: "I didn't bring any. Like my pictures, they don't do me justice!"

REMEMBRANCES

Speaker at sales convention: "Loosen up, men! While you're away from home, send the girl of your dreams a box of candy today, better still send one to your wife too!"

REPUTATION

"You make a small downpayment," said the salesman, "and then make no more payments for six months."

"Who told you about us?" demanded the lady of the house.

RESTFUL DECISION

Insurance salesman to prospect: "Don't let me frighten you into a hasty decision. Sleep on it tonight. If you wake up tomorrow, let me know then!"

RETIRED INDEBTEDNESS

If the average salesman saves for the next twenty years at the rate he's been saving for the past six months, he'll be able to retire at the age of 60 and owe only $100,000.

RETIRE SOONER

Personnel manager to job applicant: "If you prefer, you may elect to skip coffee breaks and retire three years earlier!"

REVEALING SALARY

For her first week's salary, the new secretary was given an exquisite nightgown of imported lace. The next week her "salary" was raised.

REVENGE

Housewife to door-to-door salesman: "I'll take a dozen of your most useless items. I want to get even with my husband for those books he bought the other day from a fast-talking chick!"

REVEREND DOER

The old minister was, without question, the world's worst golfer. One day on a fairly long, straight hole he uncorked a towering drive dead to the pin. The ball hit the hard turf and began rolling. As if it were drawn on by a magnet, it continued to roll.

The ball reached the apron, crossed it, then headed over the green straight for the flag. With it's last shudder of momentum, it dropped into the cup.

The astounded clergyman turned his eyes supplicatingly toward heaven, "Father, please," he pleaded, "I'd rather do it myself!"

REVERSED ATTRIBUTES

The salesman used to say that the girl he would marry will be an economist in the kitchen, an aristocrat in the living room and a harlot in bed.

Now he's married and his wife has all the traits he required, but not in his original order. She's an aristocrat in the kitchen, a harlot in the living room, an economist in bed.

RIGHT ATTITUDE

A sidewalk superintendent who had been watching two carpenters at work asked one of them, "What are you making?"

"I'm making a lousy $80 a week!" one carpenter said.

He asked the other carpenter what he was making and he replied, "I'm building a majestic edifice of worship!"

The latter had the right attitude. Unfortunately he was fired—they were both building a garage!

RIGHT BRAND

Executive to secretary after stopping on a lonely road: "I guess we're out of gas."

The secretary opened her purse and pulled out a bottle.

Executive: "Wow! You've got a whole fifth. What kind is it?"

Secretary: "Esso Plus!"

RIGHT PARTY

A sexy-looking female pollster was canvassing the neighborhood in a straw vote on the coming local election.

"May I see the gentleman of the house?" she asked.

"No," snapped the woman.

"But, I only wanted to know what party he belongs to."

"Well, take a good look. I'm the party!" the wife snapped.

RIGHT PRICE

The volunteer speaker in his opening remarks stated: "This will be a free speech and when I have finished, you will know that the price is right."

ROMANTIC CLOSES

One specialty salesman of silverware, as he nears his close, places his gleaming silver place setting on black velvet display pads on the dining room table, lights two candles, and turns out the lights. In the romantic atmosphere which he has thus created, he makes his final pitch.

He tells the prospect housewife, "Madame, there are three eventfull moments in every woman's life: when the man she loves tells her he loves her and wants to marry her, when she holds her first-born in her arms, and finally when she looks down on her first sterling silver table service. Sign here, madame. Please use this pencil and press hard, there are four carbons."

RUN-AWAY TEACHER

Deacon: "Did you hear about Ernie, the bank cashier, stealing $50,000 and running away with the president's wife?"

Minister: "Good heavens, who will teach Sunday School class tomorrow?"

RUNNING CHARGE

"I lost $75 at the race track today," the salesman lamented to another salesman in the hotel lobby.

"Don't fret," hinted his companion, "just put it on your expense account."

"What will I charge it up to?"

"Running expenses."

S

SALES BIT

A salesman's small son returned home with twenty-two dollars after selling magazine subscriptions.

Father: "How many sales did you have to make to collect that much money?"

Young salesman: "I sold all the subscriptions to one man. His dog bit me!"

SALES BUT NO SALES MEETINGS

The wife was asked how her husband was doing in his new wholesale business.

Wife: "Tremendous, but he's miserable about it!" "How come?"

Wife: "He's so busy selling and shipping, he doesn't have time to hold sales meetings."

SALES-LESS HABIT

We make our habits and then our habits make us. Take the inept salesman and his selling habits that make him inept.

He starts his "selling" day by having a coffee break and justifies not making his first call until after ten o'clock, because the customer is reading his mail.

He goes to lunch at eleven-thirty so he can beat the crowd at the luncheonette. He doesn't make his second sales call until after two-thirty, to be sure that the customer has returned from lunch.

At three-thirty, he stops in the nearest bar for a "short beer." After all he has to give his customer a chance to sign his mail.

So the inept salesman has made only two calls, consequently, his bad selling habits makes him a marginal salesman, a truly inept salesman.

SALES MANAGER WITHOUT PORTFOLIO

Executive in psychiatrist's office: "Doc, I'm in bad shape. I dislike selling. I can't sell at all. As a matter of fact, I don't know anything about selling."

Doctor: "You don't have a problem, just get out of sales."
Executive: "I can't, I'm the sales manager!"

SALES MANUAL

"I'm reading a book titled *Easy Sales,* but I don't know what to do with the other twenty copies the salesman talked me into buying!"

SALES POLITICS

Angry salesman to sales manager: "How do you expect me to respect you? You're only a political appointee."
Chagrined sales manager: "Why do you refer to me as a politician?"
Salesman: "Just like a politician, you explain nothing, deny everything, demand proof, don't listen and attack all of us!"

SALES TIMING

The vice president in charge of sales was complimenting his sales organization at the final convention dinner meeting. "I'm proud of the record you have made this past year, averaging a sale every three minutes!"

A voice rang out from the audience, "That's not fast enough."

The veep answered the dissenter by saying, "Whoever you are, please note this: with the sales campaign we're planning for next year, this sales organization will surely be making sales at the rate of one every minute and a half!"

"That's still not enough!" the dissenter cried.

"Please explain why you think so," the exasperated V.P. said.

"Because there's a sucker born every minute!"

SAME OLD PITCH

A salesman called on his purchasing agent time and time again. He finally said, "Mr. Curry, no matter how many times I come back here I always get the same old story."

The purchasing agent replied, "Look at it from my point of view. One of the main reasons you haven't got an order is that every time you've called on me, you've told me the same old story, same old sales pitch in the same old way, by the salesman who looks the same old way."

SAND WORSHIPPER

First Executive: "Who'd you play golf with?"

Second Executive: "Oh you know, him again!"

First Executive: "But you don't like him. Why'd you play with him?"

Second Executive: "Who says I don't like him? I worship the very sand-traps he walks into!"

SATISFACTORY REFERENCES

The sales manager interviewing several candidates for a job as salesmen asked a new applicant, "Have you any letter of reference?"

"I sure have," replied the salesman, "read this."

The boss put on his glasses and read the following: "To whom it may concern; John Jones worked for us one week, and we are satisfied."

SAVES 125%

The compact car craze is getting out of hand altogether. Yesterday we heard about an economy model with a new carburetor that saves 80% on gas consumption, new spark plugs that save 15% on gas consumption and a new fuel pump that saves 30% on gas consumption. In fact, if you drive the thing over 50 miles, the gas tank overflows, and you have to stop and pump the tank out!

SCORELESS RUNS

A baseball manager told his star slugger who was in a prolonged slump, "My wife's had more runs in her panty-hose than you've scored so far!"

SEAL OF DISAPPROVAL

Shopping for a suit at the shopping center men's store, the young man seemed to like the one he was trying on, but was undecided.

A salesman noticing his hesistancy inquired, "It's the style you wanted, isn't it?"

"Yes, it's cool!" the youth replied.

"It fits you well, don't you agree?" the salesman asked.

"Fits groovy!"

"Then why can't you make up your mind?"

The youth paused and said, "I'll make a deal with you. Let me take the suit home to see if my parents like it. If they do, I'll bring it back."

SECOND THOUGHT

The fun-loving salesman commented, "When I finish early making my calls, give me my golf clubs, the fresh air and a glamorous gal. On second thought, keep the golf clubs and the fresh air."

SECRETARIAL TEAMWORK

A secretary was hospitalized and one of the other girls in her office visited her. During the visit, the office friend told her to relax, not to worry about the office, and get well.

"We are sharing your work," she comforted. "Mary is making the coffee, Ruth is taking up the birthday and wedding gift collections, and I'm working the cross-word puzzles."

SEEING IS BELIEVING

Returning home very late one night, a man alibied that he had been out with his sales manager.

"That's nice," said the wife. "He's waiting for you in the living room."

"Well," snorted the man, "Who you gonna believe—me or your eyes?"

SELECTED BREAKAGE

After a toy purchase, the sales clerk inquired, "Madam, shall I wrap it up or would your son prefer to break it here?"

SELF-EFFACING

His secretary was very efficient. She always manages to be out of the office when his wife visits!

SELF-IMPROVEMENT

A woman who applied for a home improvement loan was asked what improvements she planned around the house.

"First thing, I'll get a divorce!"

SELF INCRIMINATING

She: "Why don't you play golf with Stan Roberts anymore?"
Salesman: "Would you play golf with a man who cheats, who falsifies his score and picks up his ball when your back is turned?"
She: "Of course not."
Salesman: "Well, neither will Stan Roberts."

SELF-MADE SALESMAN

The salesman claimed he was a self-made man, but added, if he had to do it all over again, he surely would call in an architect, then make the same mistakes sooner.

SELF-PRESERVATION

He's not the ordinary, garden variety drunk. Far from it. Last year he donated his body to science, so he's preserving it in alcohol till they use it.

SELF-RETIREMENT

An insurance salesman sold me a retirement policy plan. If I keep up the payments for ten years, *he retires!*

SELLER NOT A USER

The customer in the barber's chair after being asked if he wanted some hair tonic put on his hair, admonished the barber for having the nerve to sell hair tonic, when he himself, didn't even have a single hair on the top of his head.

The barber replied, "So what, I have a customer who has made a million selling brassieres!"

SELL FROM THE TOP

Housewife to door-to-door salesman: "Have you ever sold wigs?"
Salesman: "Never."
Housewife: "Here, take this one and start selling it to me. Here comes my husband!"

SELLING EXAMPLE

A salesman went to visit a local haberdashery in search of a shirt. In the store, he encountered a small, balding clerk who proved so helpful and co-operative that the salesman wound up buying three shirts and a tie. He couldn't help but admire the clerk's technique, and promptly told him, "Mister, you certainly know your merchandise and you don't treat customers as though they were blundering idiots."

"Thank you," the clerk said shyly. "Would you mind telling that to the manager on your way out? He's right over there."

The manager listened intently as the salesman repeated his compliment. "The eager beaver," he muttered, shaking his head. "You're the sixth customer he's sent to me this morning with the same story. He's making us all look bad, including me!"

"Well, what's wrong with that?" the salesman asked.

"Plenty," the manager replied. "He owns the joint!"

SELLING IS NOT FOR THE BIRDS

The new salesman reported to his sales manager that, on his first call, he had succeeded in seeing the buyer of a company that they had never been able to see before. Although he didn't get an order, as yet, he considered this a feather in his cap.

For weeks, similar reports were made. No sales, many interviews and "more feathers in his cap."

Finally, the sales manager responded with this telegram: "Your travel expense account cancelled. Take feathers from cap. Form wings. Fly home."

SELLING PRACTICE

Sales trainee to sales manager of an appliance store: "That's the last time I'm going to practice my sales talk in front of my wife!"

Sales manager: "Why?"

Sales trainee: "Now, I've got to bring home a new garbage disposal!"

SELL WAY OUT

A prisoner serving in the Danbury Federal Penitentiary, upon the completion of a course in salesmanship, went to the sales trainer and thanked him profusely. The sales trainer asked him his age.

Prisoner: "68 years old."

Sales trainer: "How long will you be here?"

Prisoner: "For life."

Sales trainer: "Why did you take this course?"

Prisoner: "If I'm ever going to get out of here, I've got to know how to sell."

SENATE PRAYERS

A salesman took his young son who had expressed a wish to be a politician when he grows up, to Washington to watch the Senate in session. The boy spotted the chaplain seated in the corner of the chamber.

"Daddy, is the chaplain there to pray for the senators?"

The salesman answered, "The truth is, the chaplain looks at the senators and then prays for the country!"

SEPARATE GYRATIONS

In today's dances, couples don't go near each other and never touch. One salesman and his wife have been doing that for years.

SEVEN-UP

Prospect: "You're lucky, I've already refused seven insurance salesmen!"

Insurance salesman: "I know, I'm them—all seven!"

SEX CLOSES

A mattress salesman in a department store, when selling to a young couple with children, always closes a sale by just casually laying his hand on the mattress, pressing on it gently and saying these words: "They are absolutely noiseless!"

Then, when he has an unmarried couple, he closes by saying, "The best for love or money!"

SEX-LESS FRIDAYS

The salesman was not feeling too hot, so he went to the doctor for a check-up. The routine examination revealed nothing, so the doctor decided to do some personal questioning.

Doctor: How often do you have sex?"

Salesman: "Every Monday, Tuesday and Friday, regularly."

Doctor: "Maybe your problem is in this area. I suggest you cutout Fridays."

Salesman: "Gosh, doctor, I can't do that. That's the only night of the week I'm home."

SEXY BALLADEER

The executive was told by his doctor that he would have to give up liquor, singing and sex.

Executive: "Doc, I can't do that!"
Doctor: "Why can't you?"
Executive: "I sing dirty drinking songs."

SEXY DOOR OPENER

Door-to-door salesman confronted at the door by a sexy-looking housewife: "May I speak to your husband?"
Mrs. Sex: "Sorry, he's on a selling trip and won't be back for another week."
Mr. Wolf: "May I come in?"

SEXY INSURANCE SALESMAN

We know an insurance salesman, who says his greatest successes are with young housewives who aren't *adequately covered!*

SHOELACES UP

A successful businessman, on his way to his office each morning, passed an old man who, for years, had stationed himself on a midtown corner selling shoelaces.

Tender-hearted, the businessman gave this old fellow a dime every morning, but took no laces. This had gone on for years.

But one Monday morning, when the daily gift of a dime was extended, the shoelace seller spoke up with more than just his usual, "Thank you." Instead he said, "I'm terribly sorry, sir, but the price of laces has gone up to 15 cents."

SHOESTRING INVESTMENT

"I just met a guy who went into business on a shoe string and tripled his investment. But what's he going to do with three shoe strings?"

SHOPPING FOR A FRIEND

Shopping for yard goods in the department store, the hard-to-please woman had been shown almost everything but was still dissatisfied. Finally she said, "Thank you, but really I'm just shopping for a friend!"

"Well," said the tired clerk, "there's still one bolt of cloth that you haven't seen, do you think she could be in there?"

SHOPPING STRATEGY

When a woman asks to see something more expensive, she's shopping. When she asks to see something cheaper, she's buying.

SHORT-SIGHTED EXAMINATION

Secretary, who had broken her glasses, asked her optician, "Will I have to be examined all over—again?"

The optician replied, "No, just your eyes."

SHOW-OFFS

Why is it that sales clerks who never know the price of anything and hold your purchase in the air, asking every other sales clerk the price, work in the lingerie department?

SICK SALES

A salesman's sales soared unexpectedly because of illness in his family. His wife was "sick" of having nothing to wear.

SICK WASHER

Women spend most of the money in our country today on things like wash-day products. I heard of a woman who took all the wash-day products in her confusion and threw them in the machine at the same time—new blue detergent, old pink detergent, middle-aged green detergent, detergent with enzymes, tablet bleach, water softener. It all came shooting out again.

She told the repairman, "My washer broke down."

He replied, "Madam, your washer did not break-down—it threw up!"

SIDELINE

The inept salesman has something going on the side for him—his wife works!

SIGNATURE OF INDEPENDENCE

A junior account executive was drowning his sorrows one night in a tavern because his boss, a rough type, had fired him for no reason at all. It happened just after the boss had sent some prints of the Declaration of Independence to be put on the walls.

"What's wrong with that?" the young man was asked.

"I dunno," was his reply. "All I did was read it, add my name to the bottom, and pass it on!"

SIGNS OF TIME

Inept salesman says: "I'm sure that business is picking up. I'm starting to lose bigger sales!"

SIMPLE MARK-UP

Two graduates of the class of '45 met on the campus upon the occasion of their twentieth reunion. One had just stepped out of his multi-cylinder sports job. His big cigar, the obviously expensive suit, and the gleaming diamonds left no doubt about this old grad's worldy status.

"Great to see ya, Bob," he greeted his seedy-looking erstwhile classmate. "Often wondered about you—the boy who never got less than 'A' plus in any subject. Howya doin?"

"Just fair," was the reply, "I find they don't pay for past performance. But you look like you've done all right. How many banks do you own?"

"Well, I've done O.K.," said the other. "I was never a brain like you and I knew it. In fact, I flunked math and had to take something else. So when I got out of school I figured I better get into something simple. And I did. I found an item I could buy for $1 and sell for $5, and believe me Bob, over the years that four per cent mounts up!"

SITS AND SOUNDS OFF

The sportsman went to a hunting lodge and bagged a record number of birds with the help of a dog named "Salesman." The following year, the man wrote the lodge again for reservations, requesting the same dog, "Salesman."

As soon as he arrived at the lodge, he asked the handler if "Salesman" was to hunt.

"Hound ain't no durn good now," the handler said.

"What happened?" cried the man. "Was he injured?"

"Nope! Some fool came down here and called him 'Sales Manager' all week. Now all he does is sit on his tail and bark."

SIZING THE PURCHASE

The salesman, who was in a ladies store, couldn't remember his wife's measurements. He looked around for a sales girl built approximately as his wife. One was too tall. Another was too short, but a nearby shopper was nearly built like his wife, so he said, "Excuse me, sir, what size are you?"

SIZZLING NOISE

After a night on the town, a hung-over salesman was asked if he wanted an Alka-Selzer.

He replied, "Oh no! I won't be able to stand the sizzling!"

SLUMPING EXECUTIVE

After the executive had slumped in his office chair from a too liquid lunch, his secretary answered his phone announcing, "I'm sorry, he's out *from* lunch."

SMALLER STICKING

The auto salesman asked me if I wanted a Dodge Dart or the American Motor's Javelin?

I said, "I'd rather get stuck with a Dart than a Javelin anytime!"

"SMALLER THAN A BREADBOX?"

A group of salesmen were discussing and wondering what the manager's assistant did for his salary.

One spoke up and said, "Do you know the boss is wondering, too. That's why he's trying to get him on 'What's My Line.' "

SMELLY DAD

Sales of after-shave lotions and deodorants for men were at an alltime high for Father's Day. Does this prove that pop is beginning to stink?

SMILING OPINIONATED EXECUTIVE

The manager who can smile when things go wrong has probably just thought of someone he can blame it on.

He's the guy who says, "When I want your opinion, I'll give it to you!"

He also says, "You have a right to your opinion, as long as it agrees with mine!"

SOMETHING NEW ADDED

I understand that a detergent has been added to Geritol. It's for dirty old men!

SOUTHERN HOSPITALITY

A Florida motel wakes up it's guests who leave morning calls, not by phone but by sending a maid with a pot of coffee for breakfast.

A salesman who came in late one night, put in a phone call to his home and then decided it was too late, and cancelled it. He had to leave early the next morning and so he left a call with the ·switchboard operator.

In the morning the girl had just arrived with coffee, when his room phone rang. The salesman, still half asleep, motioned for the girl to answer it. So she did. "Oh, yes, indeed, he's right heah in bed," she said in a rich Southern accent, "Ah'll put him on."

The call, of course was from the salesman's wife in Chicago.

SPACE SELLING

Ad salesman to publisher: "You think these astronauts have a tough job? All they have to do is explore space. I have to sell it!"

SPEAKERS DILEMMA

The executive swings confidently into the climax of his ghost written speech and says, "Now let me tell you what we should do about it."

He then turns to the last page of text and finds, scrawled: "All right wise guy—you're on your own!"

SPEECHES OF FIRE

Sales speaker: "Should I put more fire in some of my talks?"
Critic: "No, vice versa! Put more of your talks in the fire."

SPEECHLESS PART

The budding young actor burst into his father's study.

"Dad, guess what? I've got my first part in a play," he sputtered. "I play the part of a man who has been married 35 years."

"That's a good start, son," replied the father. "Just keep at it and one of these days you'll get a speaking part."

SPEEDY TOLL BOOTHS

Traveling salesmen, today, can't decide whether they're driving faster now, or whether they're putting the toll booths closer together!

SPELLING ASSISTANT

The nicest thing about being an executive and dictating your letter is that you can use words you can't spell!

SPELLING INSTEAD OF SELLING

The newly hired traveling salesman wrote his first sales report to the home office. It stunned the brass in the sales department. Obviously, the new "hope" was a blithering illiterate, for here's what he had written:

"I seen this outfit which they ain't never bought a dime's worth of nothing from us and I sole them a couple hundred thousand dollars of guds. I am now going to Chcawgo."

But before the illiterate itinerant could be given the heave-ho by the sales manager, along came another letter: "I cum hear and sole them haff a millyon."

Fearful if he did; and fearful if he didn't fire the illiterate peddler, the sales manager decided to dump the problem in the lap of the president. The following morning, the members of the ivory tower were flabbergasted to see the two letters posted on the bulletin board and this letter from the president tacked above:

"We ben spending two much time trying to spel instead of trying to sel. Lets wach those sails. I want everbody should read these letters from Gooch who is on the rode doing a grate job for us, and you should go out and do like he done!"

SPIRITED QUESTION

The traveling salesman was intrigued with the message on the motel's desk sign. It read: "Double Room, Breakfast, Lunch, Floor Show and Bottle of Scotch—only $5.00.

The motel manager noticed the look of scepticism on the salesman's face, so he asked him, "Don't you believe it's for real?"

The salesman replied, "I have a question. Is it a pint or quart of scotch?"

SPORTY MORAL

The football season is the only time of the year when a man can walk down the street with a blonde on one arm and a blanket on the other without encountering raised eyebrows.

SPORTY OFFER

Busy B-girl at bar: "Bill, you can come over about seven-ish, you George, around eight-ish. Frank, I'll have time for you around nine-ish."

She then spun around on her bar stool and asked, "Ten-ish, anyone?"

STAGGERING CERTAINTY

A cop saw a staggering drunk in front of a house and asked, "Are you sure this is your house?"

"Shertainly, and if you'll just open the door f'me, I'll prove it to you," he sputtered.

"You shee that piano, thash mine. You shee that T.V. set, thash mine, too. Follow me. Thish ish my bedroom. Shee that bed, shee that woman lying in the bed, thash my wife and shee that guy lying next to her? Yeah! Thash me!"

STARLET STICK-UP

I once knew a gorgeous and absolutely stunning girl, who always wanted to be a movie star. But one small problem kept holding her back. Her measurements were 26-40-26. She looked like an inside-out Raquel Welch. So, to tide herself over, she got a job as a teller in a Hollywood bank.

The first day a robber came in, pointed a gun at her and said: "Stick 'em up!"

She just ignored him.

He repeated, "Stick 'em up!"

She ignored him.

"Didn't you hear me? I said, stick 'em up!"

She finally answered, "If I could, I'd be in pictures!"

STATUS BARGAIN

Lady to gift store clerk: "Do you have a birthday gift for a junior executive that has lots of status in a quiet and unassuming way, for about $5.00?"

STICK-UP SERVICE

Notice in the *Boston Globe:* "To the bank robbers who broke into our River Branch, First National Bank offers complete banking service at all of our offices. Next time you have a financial problem, let one of our trained loan officers assist you."

STIFF REASON

Show me a sales executive who walks with his head high and erect, and I'll show you a sales executive with a stiff neck.

STINGING PROBLEM

Returning to a desk piled-up with an accumulation of things to do after a vacation, is like being a mosquito in a nudist camp. There's so much to be done that you don't know where to start.

STOCKING DEMONSTRATOR

A salesman who sold ladies stockings was discussing his selling technique to a back-fence neighbor. "If the women are interested, I put them on for them."

"You must see lots of pretty legs!"

"No, my legs look lousy in women's hose."

STOCK'S INTERRUPTIONS

Two salesman, expectant fathers, met in the waiting room of the hospital.

"What a tough break," said one. "This had to happen during my vacation."

"You think you've got a tough break," said the other. "I'm on my honeymoon!"

STOMACH INSURANCE

Personnel director to applicant: "It's the type of job that may give you ulcers, but Blue Cross covers that nicely."

STOP BUYING!

A big store buyer kept wiring his wife each week, for the past six weeks: "Can't come home yet. Stop. Still buying. Stop."

On the sixth week, his wife wired in reply: "Better come home. Stop. Or I'll start selling what you are buying. Stop."

STORE'S BENEFACTOR

As a sales clerk was carrying an armload of imported china, he tripped. The expensive dishes smashed on the floor of the department store, before scores of shocked customers. From the group emerged a distinguished-looking gentleman.

"I suppose that the store will take the loss out of your pay check," he said.

"Yes," the clerk sighed. "I'll be months paying off the breakage."

"Well," said the gentleman, turning to the crowd, "why don't we take up a collection for this poor young man? Only a dollar or so apiece will help." He collected more than $60, turned it over to the clerk and then vanished.

"What a fine man," said a touched onlooker.

"Yes," said the clerk, "and he's a pretty smart store manager, too."

STORK WINNER

A dress shop received this note from a woman: "Dear Sir, you have not delivered the maternity dress I ordered. Please cancel the order. My delivery was faster than yours."

STRAIGHT FROM THE SHOULDER

"It was a great speech Mayor, I liked the straight forward way you dodged the issues!"

The mayor should have approached matters with an open mind instead of an open mouth.

STRANGE BRINGING-UP

The salesman just couldn't take his teen-age daughter's appearance any longer. He marched her to the bathroom and washed all the make-up off her face and combed back all her hair, then cried out, "So help me, I've been bringing up somebody else's kid!"

STRANGE WALLOPPER

One traveling salesmen, being on the road so much and away from home, experienced difficulty in disciplining his children when he was home.

For instance, one Sunday afternoon he was intensely watching a championship football game on T.V. His son came into the room and started making so much noise that the father missed seeing the championship touchdown. He was so upset, that he walloped his son. The boy started to cry and ran to the kitchen to his mother, who asked, "What are you crying for?"

The son cried, "That bald-headed guy who stays here on Sunday just hit me."

STRANGER IN THE NIGHT

Traveling salesman to motel clerk: "I'd like a room with a bath for my wife and myself."

Motel clerk: "Sorry, but we only have rooms without baths available at the present."

Salesman: "Will that be all right, dear?"

Dear: "Sure, Mister!"

STRETCHED OPINION

A salesman at a sales convention nudged the salesman sitting next to him and pointed to a man coming into the room.

Salesman: "That's the principal speaker for today. I heard him at our last convention and he had us all in the aisles."

Newcomer: "Applauding?"

Salesman: "No, stretching and yawning."

STRIKING OUT VIA WESTERN UNION

A traveling salesman who was selling more but making less wired his sales manager: "Deserve raise. Need it big, in two weeks or else strike me out."

His sales manger wired back: "Strike one. Strike two. Strike three and you're out!"

STRUCK OUT!

The salesman's wife was so cold one night that she put on their son's baseball uniform, including the stocking, but he didn't even get to first base.

STUPID QUERY

A fellow catches his wife in the back seat of a car with another man and shouts: "What's going on in there?"

His wife turns to her lover and says, "See, I told you he was stupid!"

SUBURBAN PRAYERS

Prayer by a weary suburbanite: "Keep my neighbors, please oh Lord, from buying things I can't afford!"

SUCCESSFUL CLIMBING

It's easier to climb the ladder of success in business if your father owns the ladder.

SUCCESSFUL FAILURE

The inept salesman was telling a friend, "Since my company has put me on straight commission, I'm selling more."

And he is—last week his furniture, this week his house and next week his car! You could call him a successful failure!

SUCCESSFUL NEPOTISM

Chairman of the board to his son: "Don't think you're coming in the business and starting at the top! You'll begin as a vice president, just like your uncle and I did!

"Remember too, I didn't get where I am overnight—it took months to probate your grandfather's will!"

SUCCESSFUL SALESMAN

The president called in the personnel manager and instructed him to get a customer relations man, an experienced engineer, a skilled diplomat, a dedicated problem solver, a persuasive speaker, a marketing expert and a credit consultant.

Personnel manager: "O.K. I'll place seven want ads in the Sunday News."

President: "I don't want seven men. I need and want a *successful salesman!"*

SUCCESS WAS IN THE BAG

Mr. Big Wheel was deeply touched when he arose to speak, at the testimonial dinner given in honor of his fiftieth anniversary. His voice trembled when he spoke.

"When I came to this city," he said, "I walked down the dusty street. I had no fine automobile, not even a horse and buggy. My only suit was on my back and the soles of my shoes were getting thin. All my personal possessions I carried in a brown paper sack.

"Our city has been good to me. My store has prospered. I own a newspaper and radio station. I'm president of our largest bank and I hold controlling interest in a corporation that operates stores in 257 cities. I'm a member of our leading clubs and I own several business blocks."

After the dinner, Mr. Big Wheel was approached by a lad who shyly asked, "Mister, could you tell me what you carried in that brown paper sack when you came here fifty years ago?"

"Sure son, I can recall every item. In that bag I had $200,000 in cash and $300,000 in negotiable bonds."

SUGGESTED ULTIMATUM

Sales manager to salesman: "I have a suggestion to make about a change in our sales policy for the coming year. I'd like opinions from all of you. Those opposed to my ideas will signify by saying, 'I resign!' "

SUPERMARKET TRAFFIC JAM

If you think a woman driving a car can snarl traffic, you ought to see a man pushing a cart in the supermarket!

SUPER-SALESMANSHIP

He's the kind of a salesman who could sell a suit and a topcoat to a shopper who only wanted to buy two pair of shoe laces; who can sell a new widow shopping for a suit for her husband's funeral, a black suit with two pair of pants.

SUPPLY AND DEMAND

Successful marriages of over twenty years are usually based on good business standards, the law of supply and demand. The wives demand and the husbands supply.

SUPPRESSING EVIDENCE

The judge asked the salesman who was trying to be excused from jury duty, "You're trying to tell this court that your firm can't do without you?"

The salesman quickly answered, "No, your honor. They can, but I don't want them to find out."

SURPRISE GIFT

The sales executive walked into the stationary store and said to the sales clerk, "Please show me your better line of fountain pens. I would like something extra special. It's for my wife's birthday."

The sales clerk asked with a knowing glance, "A little surprise?"

"Quite," the executive said, "She's expecting a Thunderbird."

SUSPICIOUS DINNER

The salesman suspected that the stewardess didn't like him. When he ordered dinner she asked, "Will that be to take out?"

SWINGING SPENDER

Sales executive to swinging salesman: "You must concentrate all your imagination, initiative and energies into your expense account!"

T

TAKE-OUT SERVICE?

After a $10 purchase of groceries, the check-out attendant asked, "Is this to go or will you eat it here?"

TAKES TEAMWORK

"Why does it take three of your guys to change a burned out light bulb?" asked the foreman.

"Well," retorted the assistant, "Jim holds the bulb while Frank and I turn the ladder."

TARDINESS

The bright young sales trainee was a ball of fire in training sessions and on his initial calls, indicating that he would go far. However, he had one fault that so provoked the sales manager that he called him into his office to discuss it with him.

"Young man," said the sales executive, "I'm tired of your being late every morning, whether it is to attend a session or to go out on a call. If you're going to grow into the sort of salesman we want around here, you must overcome your tardiness. To teach you a lesson, I am going to suspend you for two days without pay. When would you like to take them?"

"Well, if it's all the same with you," he answered, "I'd like to use up the days by being late."

TAX CUT

Did you hear about the Medicare patient who had surgery? He woke up and found a placard on his incision with: "This is a Federal project showing your tax dollars at work."

TAX DEDUCTABLE

Then there's the home builder who bought his wife a bra and deducted it from his income tax. He called it a structural improvement!

TEAM STRIKES OUT

The teamsters want to organize professional sports. I can see it now. It's the top of the 7th and a manager sends his pitcher to the showers. As the reliever comes in the rest of the team yell "Scab!"

TEARFUL STRATEGY

The sales manager called in his best salesman and laid down the strategy.

Sales manager: "Even though business is slow all over, I want you to go on the road and hustle up some sales."

Salesman: "Why have me go out in the field to sell, at a time like this? To get any sales, I'll have to cry and soften their hearts."

Sales manager: "That's what I want you to do—cry and shed some real tears."

So off went the salesman, but five weeks later he came back without one order.

Sales manager: "What? Not even a single sale. Did you cry and cry like I instructed you to do?"

Salesman: "Did I cry! I let the tears pour out! I didn't sell anything, but I got eighty-five dollars for myself."

TELL ME MORE

The high-pressure salesman had taken a behavior pattern test and now his sales manager was giving him the results.

Sales manager: "The test has catalogued you as being egotistical, argumentative, self-centered, easily irritated, hostile, having a fast fuse and pushing people to the wall. Do you have any questions?"

Salesman: "Yes, now tell me the bad things!"

TEMPORARY NAME PLATE

The executive knew immediately that he was on his way out when he noticed that his name was scotch-taped on his desk.

$10,000 MOTIVE

Husband: "I just bought another $10,000 policy."
Wife: "Oh, I could kill you!"

$10,000 QUESTION

The man-about-town and his attractive blonde companion were seated at a table in a plush restaurant. Suddenly he glanced cautiously about, then turned to the blonde and whispered, "I've a question for you, honey. Could you care for a man who had swindled his firm out of ten thousand dollars?"

The young lady also looked cautiously about the room, then looking him squarely in the eye, said, "And I've a question for you. Have you still got it?"

TESTING ALL EXECUTIVES

The executive took the aptitude test along with his salesmen. After getting the results, he exclaimed, "Thank heavens, I own the company!"

THANKFUL VOTER

A man-on-the street interviewer sought opinions on the approaching election. He asked one old fellow what he thought of the two candidates.

"When I look at them," the retired executive replied, "I'm thankful only one of them can get elected!"

THAWED ILLNESS

The doctor diagnosed the sales executive's illness as Hydropsy.
Executive: "Come again in plain English."
Doctor: "Too much water in the body."
Executive: "Come off of it, Doc! I never drink water, but it must be that ice!"

THINKING ANEW

Assistant sales manager to his wife: "We had a tough day at the office. The computer broke down and everyone had to think!"

THINKING EMBEZZLER

The brazen robber shoved the meek bank clerk aside and began scooping up the money. Then, the quivering little man said, "Please take the books too. I'm $5,000 short!"

THINK POSITIVELY

A very capable salesman shifted into high gear and made certain that he won first prize in his company's sales contest. It was a Caribbean cruise for himself and his wife. His accomplishment was well publicized at the national sales meeting, in the house organ and sales bulletins.

Then came the day for he and his wife to go on the trip. When they boarded the ship in New York, they noted that the company had cut a few corners. They realized that they were not traveling first class. How could they tell? There wasn't any lavatory in the stateroom. But they looked around and discovered a fine lavatory at the end of the passageway. This was certainly acceptable and, as positive thinkers, settled down for the night looking forward to a good time.

In the middle of the night, the wife awakened, deathly ill. She was so seasick that she was green. She could only think of one thing—the lavatory at the end of the passageway. So she leaped out of her bunk, stormed through the stateroom door and headed for the lavatory. Halfway down the passageway, she bumped into a man, a negative thinker, with the very same problem.

At that very moment she realized that she was completely nude and she shrieked.

"Don't worry, lady," the man exclaimed, "I won't live to tell anybody!"

THOUGHTFUL PRICING

There lives an obstetrician in Buffalo who has two fixed charges. He sends patients a bill for either $100 or $200.

"Do you look up your patients' financial rating before you decide on your charge?" he was asked one day by a friend.

"Not at all," answered the doctor. "I have my fee on the first question the father asks, when I come out of the delivery room. If he asks, 'Is it a boy or a girl?' he gets a bill for $200. But if he asks, 'Is my wife all right?' I only bill him for $100."

THOUGHTFULNESS

A couple were checking into a hotel. After a generous tip, the bell hop asked, "Will there be anything else, sir?"

"No thanks," the salesman said.

"Anything for your wife, sir?"

After a minute of thought the salesman replied, "Why yes, come to think of it, bring me a postcard to send to her."

THREATENED!

The salesman was asked, "How long have you worked for this company?"

"Ever since they threatened to fire me!" he replied.

TICKLISH SECRETARY

Executive after interviewing prospective secretary: "Where can I get hold of you?"

Secretary: "I don't know, I'm ticklish all over!"

TIME DIFFERENCE

The strike was still on, although management and labor had agreed to a 50 cent increase. Management offered it by the hour. Labor wanted it by the minute.

TIMELY SUGGESTION

During a dragged-out campaign speech, the candidate looked at his watch, then absent-mindedly put it to his ear.

A heckler responded, "Charlie if your watch has stopped running, there's a calendar on the wall behind you."

TIMES AT BAT

A male patient went to his psychiatrist and told the doctor that all he ever dreamed about was baseball.

The doctor asked, "Don't you ever dream about a beautiful girl—wining her, dining her and holding her tight? Listen, didn't you ever dream about girls?"

"What?" screamed the patient. "And lose my turn at bat?"

TIME TO BUY

An auto salesman told his customer, "Do you realize that while you're standing here dickering, your car is depreciating?"

TIRED LAST WORDS

The speaker told the program chairman, "After my talks, I get home too tired for words, but my wife insists on talking anyway."

TIRED SNAKE

"Driest town I ever saw, was in Kansas," said one salesman to another salesman, as they discussed prohibition.

"They couldn't sell liquor there at all?" asked his friend.

"Only if you had been bitten by a snake," said the first salesman. "They only had one snake in town. When I got to it one day, after standing in line more than 12 hours, I near died of thirst. It was too tired to bite!"

TOASTING THE AUTHOR

Lady to an author, autographing his book in department store: "I've decided to give your book to my aunt for her birthday—a toaster costs too much."

TOGETHERNESS

Two heavy drinking salesmen met.

First salesman: "Man, I tried in every way to get in touch with you last night. I called your office and you had left. I called your home, they said you hadn't come home as yet. Where were you?"

Second salesman: "I was with you!"

TOLERANT ARRANGEMENTS

A salesman who had just won a sales trip to Las Vegas, wired the hotel he was to stay at: "Can you make arrangements so I can put up with my wife?"

TOPIC-HAPPY CHAIRMAN

The Rotary Club program chairman gave the next month's speaker a list of six topics to speak on.

The speaker retorted, "Six topics? You don't want a speaker, you want a committee!"

TOPICAL MINUTE

At a large public dinner, several long-winded speakers had covered almost every subject possible. When yet another speaker rose, he said, "It seems to me that everything has been talked about, but if someone will tell me what to talk about, I will be grateful."

From the back of the room a slightly inebriated man staggered to his feet and shouted, "Talk about a minute!"

TOPICLESS

A salesman who had come into the sales meeting late and in the middle of the sales manager talk asked the salesman he sat next to, "What's the boss talking about?"

The fellow salesman replied, "So far, he doesn't say."

TRAFFIC JAMMED SALES

Auto dealers are bemoaning the fact that new cars are not moving off their lots. I've got news for them. New or old cars are not moving in our city streets either!

TRAINED BUTTERFLIES

The sales speaker used to have butterflies in his stomach whenever he faced an audience. Now he knows how to make them work for him—they fly in formation.

TRAVELING LIGHT

A certain traveling salesman never takes his wife on his selling trips because he doesn't believe in taking anything with him that he doesn't need.

TRAVELING TIME

A salesman covering a large territory was complaining to his sales manager of the many hours his selling and traveling involved.

"Why," said the sales manager, "when I was out on the road I often put in 16 hours a day and thought nothing of it."

"I've been doing the same thing for weeks, and I don't think a lot of it either!" replied the salesman.

TRIPLE EFFORT

The faithful office worker of thirty years told his boss, "I've been doing three mens' work for a long time and I think I deserve a substantial raise!"

"You've been doing three mens' work?" the boss asked. "Tell me who the other two men are, and I'll fire them!"

TRIPLE PLATOONING

The ultimate in the application of the platoon system for a football squad is one platoon for offense, one platoon for defense, and one platoon to go to classes.

TROUBLES DEFERRED

"Man, you think you have troubles! Listen, I got so much trouble right now that if anything else goes wrong today, I can't possibly worry about it until ten days from now!"

TRUE TO FORM

The door-to-door salesman applying for a license at the police station answered two of the questions on the application as follows:

Sex: Occasionally
Business: Lousy.

TRYING EFFORT

Sales manager: "Charlie, I don't know how we're going to get along without you, yet on Monday, we are going to try. So, I'm firing you."

TURNED OUT SALESMAN

"Of course I have a reference," declared the inept salesman. "I sold for Macy, and here's their letter saying I'm the best salesman they ever turned out."

T.V. DINNER COMING UP

The young married salesman of a few weeks had had a really hard day at the office, and when he arrived home that evening he looked worn out. His bride was sympathetic. "Darling," she said, "you look so tired and hungry. How would you like a nice steak smothered with onions, a green vegetable, some French fried potatoes and some delicious pie-a-la-mode?"

"Not tonight, dear," was the weary husband's reply. "I'm too tired to go out."

T.V. SURVEY

A recent survey shows twice as many T.V. sets than bathtubs in American homes, proving there are a lot of dirty people watching T.V.

$25 SECRET

"I just laid out $25 for a new book, *The Secrets of Getting Rich.* Now I know the secret! Write a book that sells for $25.00!"

TWO DESK EXECUTIVES

The inept sales executive needs two desks—one for each foot to give direction to salesmen who have two feet on the ground.

TWO-FOOTED REPLY

Salesman exclaimed to his teenage son: "What do you mean, you want to borrow my car? What are your feet for?"

New generation: "One foot is for the gas pedal and one foot is for the brake pedal."

TWO-PARTY RESULTS

After the elections are over, we will still be a two-party country. The appointed and the disappointed!

TWO-WAY PRAYING

Reporter: "I understand you carry a chaplain to pray for the team."

Student manager: "That's right."

Reporter: "Would you mind introducing him to me?"

Student manager: "Be glad to. Which one, the offensive chaplain or the defensive chaplain?"

TWO-WAY PROFITEER

Here's a disturbing thought: When you buy stocks your broker makes a profit and if you panic and sell the broker still makes a profit.

U

UNANIMOUS DISLIKES

One executive strikes up a conversation with another executive at a cocktail lounge.

No. 1: "Are you Joe Smith from Continental?"
No. 2: "Yes."
No. 1: "Were you in Chicago last week?"
No. 2: "Yes."
No. 1: "Was your room number 213?"
No. 2: "Yes."
No. 1: "Did you meet Mrs. Wentworth in room number 214?"
No. 2: "Yes."
No. 1: "Well, I'm Mr. Wentworth, and I don't like it!"
No. 2: "You know, you're right, I didn't like it either!"

UNCLE SAM'S EXAMPLE

The Internal Revenue auditor said to the small businessman, "On your return you show an income of $8,000 and expenditures of $12,000. How is that possible?"

"Simple," the businessman replied, "the government does it all the time!"

UNCOMFORTABLE OR COMFORTABLE?

"I would like to see some furniture," stated the prospect.
"Modern or comfortable?" asked the salesman.

UNDERSTATEMENT

An under-financed businessman applied to his bank for a $50,000 loan. The loan officer told him, "For that kind of money, we require a statement. Can you give us one?"

"Certainly," replied the businessman, "I'm optimistic!"

UNDER WRAPS SHOPPING

Clerk: "May I help you?"
Shopper: "No, thanks, I'm only shoplifting."

UNEMPLOYED SALESMEN

To the question: "How many salesmen work for you?" the sales manager answered: "Just about half!"

To the same question another sales manager said, "Twenty four, no, I'll change that. Twenty four have territories."

UNEXPRESSED OPINION

Friend: "Don't you and your sales manager ever have a difference of opinion?"
Salesman: "Sure we do. But I don't tell him!"

UNFORGIVABLE SALE

At a late summer fur sale, a woman was overheard asking the saleslady, "Will a small deposit hold it until my husband does something unforgivable?"

UNHAPPY POP

The salesman's son told his teacher, "I come from a broken home. My dad can't repair anything!"

UNHAPPY SALARY INCREASE

The manager was reviewing the salary of his men. He asked his assistant, "How would Tom Jones feel about a $500 increase?"

The assistant replied, "He'd be unhappy with such a small increase."

The manager then inquired, "How do you think he would feel about a $1000 increase?"

"He would still be unhappy," the assistant affirmed.

"Then we'll let him be unhappy for $500."

UNKNOWN TERRITORY

One inept salesman asked another, "Where are you going?"
The other replied, "Out in the field, wherever that is!"

UNLOADING STRATEGY

An appliance distributor had 36 color T.V. stereo player combinations that just wouldn't move. None of his dealers would touch them even when he cut the price in half.

"What'll I do?" he asked a fellow distributor at a convention.

"Well," said his friend, "If I had the same problem I'd ship six sets to each of six discount houses with an invoice for five sets each. They'll think it is your mistake and will take advantage of you by accepting the shipment."

Three weeks later the distributor called his friend and blasted his ear. "Fine advice you gave me," he shouted. "Each discount house to whom I sent six sets and billed for only five, returned the five mentioned in the invoice and kept the extra one."

UNMARKETABLE

A drunk staggered into a bar. He bet the bartender that he

could tell the ingredients of any drink ever mixed. The bartender thereupon mixed the dregs of several drinks, a martini, scotch, bourbon and several liqueurs into one glass. He handed it to the drunk. The drunk carefully sipped the drink, and identified every single ingredient perfectly. He offered to do likewise with any other mixture.

This time, the bartender filled a glass with water. The drunk tasted it, meditated for a moment, then announced, "I don't know what it is. But I can tell you this, it won't sell!"

UNPREJUDICED NONSENSE

The older member of the program committee who had heard the scheduled speaker before, went to him and declared, "Even though I have heard you before, I'm not one bit prejudiced. I'm going to listen with a perfectly open and unbiased mind to what I'm convinced is pure rubbish and sheer nonsense."

UNPROTECTED MISTAKES

Too bad there's no accident insurance to protect the girl who pursues the wrong policy!

UNRECORDED HELP

Wife to husband dismayed by bank's "overdrawn" notice: "I didn't want to worry you, that's why I didn't enter those checks in the checkbook."

UNSETTLED MORNING

Traveling salesman: "Good morning. Have you ever seen anything as unsettled as this weather we've been having?"
Hotel clerk: "Well, there's your bill here!"

UNSUSPECTING SALESMAN

A woman told her friend, "I met your husband the other day. What a brilliant salesman! I suppose he knows everything."
"Don't be silly," replied the wife, "he doesn't suspect a thing!"

UNUSUAL CONTEST

One sales contest offered these prizes:
   1st prize: A week in Las Vegas.
   2nd prize: A week in Las Vegas, but with your wife.
   3rd prize: Philadelphia.

UNWORKABLE MODELS

Sales manager: "I have model salesmen. Too bad they're not working models!"

UP, UP AND AWAY

Prospect: "I've got too much insurance now!"
Salesman: "How do you know?"
Prospect: "My wife suggested I take up sky diving!"

URGENT REQUEST

A salesman phoned his bank to request a loan. The banker asked how soon he needed the money.

The salesman answered, "Well, to give you an idea, this call is collect!"

USED EVIDENCE

Having completed a quick sale the day before, a used-car salesman was somewhat worried, if not surprised, to see the purchaser driving the car back into the lot.

"What's the matter?" demanded the salesman. "There's nothing wrong with the car is there?"

"Nothing wrong," was the reply. "I just wanted to return these things for the quiet little old lady you said owned the car before I bought it. She left her panty-hose and a bottle of vodka under the seat."

V

VACATION PROBLEMS

There's only one problem when you go away for a vacation: You can turn off the gas and the electricity, but you can't turn off the mortgage payments.

VACATION STRATEGY

A vacation should be just long enough for the boss to miss you, but not long enough for him to discover he can get along without you!

VACATION TIME

A salesman snowed in by a blizzard wired the home office: "I can't get out of my hotel room in this small town for two weeks. Stop. I cannot sell anything. Stop. What shall I do?"

The sales manager replied, "Start your vacation immediately!"

VANISHING RAISE

Salesman: "May I have a raise in salary?"

Sales manager: "But I gave you a $10 increase only last month."

Salesman: "Holy cow, my wife didn't tell me!"

VARIED HOLDUP

A shrewd gunman appeared at the paymaster's window and demanded, "Never mind the payroll, Bud, just hand over the welfare fund, the group insurance premiums, the pension fund, and the withholding taxes!"

VASE OF ASHES

After gaining entrance to the prospect's home, the salesman put on his personality act. "My, what a lovely home you have," he gushed. "And, tell me, what is in the beautiful vase on the mantelpiece?"

"My husband's ashes," said the young wife.

"Oh, I'm sorry. How long has he been dead?" asked the salesman.

"He's not. He's just too lazy to find an ashtray."

VERSATILE BEGGAR

"It must be awful to be lame," said a passerby to crippled beggar.

"It is," replied the beggar.

"Wouldn't it be worse if you were blind?" asked the man.

The beggar answered, "Yes, when I was blind, people kept giving me foreign coins!"

VERSATILE SKIRTS

A mini-skirt should be long enough to cover everything, yet short enough to maintain interest in everything!

VERTIGO CLOSE

Every time the customer tried on a suit the salesman would turn him around to face the mirror. After the prospective customer had tried on every suit in his size but one, and still no sale,. the salesman turned him over to another salesman.

This salesman had the customer try on the remaining suit and made the sale.

When the customer had left the store, the successful salesman turned to his selling partner and said, "See how easy it was. I sold him on the first try."

"But," replied his partner, "who made him dizzy?"

VICE-PRESIDENTS BY THE DOZEN

The self-important stuffed shirt businessman came home from work one day, more puffed up than ever. "I've been made a vice-president of our firm," he boasted to his wife.

Thoroughly annoyed with him, considering his previous boasts, she snapped, "So what? Vice-presidents are a dime a dozen. The grocery market, where I shop, for example, has so many vice-presidents, it even has one in charge of prunes."

"Oh, yes?" said he, as he grabbed the telephone and dialed the local supermarket.

When the operator at the store answered the telephone, he said, "I'd like to speak to the vice-president in charge of prunes."

"Packaged or bulk?" she asked.

VIEW OF THE NEIGHBOR

Door-to-door salesman to housewife, answering his ring: "You should have seen what I saw at your neighbor's! May I come in?"

VIRTUE ON EARTH

Insurance salesman to farmer: "Look at it this way, how would your wife carry on if you should die?"

Farmer: "Well, I don't reckon that's any concern of mine, so long as she behaves herself while I'm alive."

VISUAL SELECTION

The sales vice-president needed a secretary and the psychologist from the personnel department invited him to watch an examination of candidates for the job.

The psychologist called in the first girl and asked, "What's two and two?"

Her answer was prompt, "Four."

The second girl thought for a moment, suspecting a catch, and said, "Twenty-two."

The last applicant answered, "Four, but it could be 22."

"The test was very revealing," explained the psychologist. "The first girl has a conventional mind; to her, two and two are always four. The second girl has imagination; she realized it might be 22. The third girl is a combination of both; she's practical and has imagination. Now which would you like?"

Without hesitation, the vice-president replied, "The one in the tight yellow sweater."

VOICE OF EXPERIENCE

Experienced stenographer to new girl: "Oh, you'll like it here. Lots of chance for advance!"

VOTE WAS 8 TO 7

The president of a machinery company, who suffered an attack while presiding at a board meeting, had this telegram delivered to him in the hospital the next day: "Board passed following resolution this morning as first order of business: 'That the Board go on record as expressing the hope and desire for a speedy and complete return to full good health by President Jones.' (Signed) B. Smith, Chairman. P.S. The vote was 8 to 7."

VOTING CHARGES

The man worked hard for his candidate during the election and was very much surprised to find himself brought into court.

"What have I been arrested for?" he inquired.

"You are charged," said the judge, "with voting seven times."

"Charged!" exclaimed the defendant. "I thought I was getting paid!"

WAITING LOAFER

Shoe department manager to customer: "Yes, we have a selection of loafers. I'll see if I can get one to wait on you!

WALK-OUT TIME

The sales speaker inquired of the club president, "How long do you want me to speak?"

The club president replied, "You can talk as long as you want to, but we adjourn at one-thirty."

WANT-AD TRAGEDY

Tragedy is answering the blind ad for a job that your boss put in the paper.

WANT VS. NEED

At a haberdashery counter a male shopper was greeted by a beautiful blonde clerk with, "Good afternoon. What can I do for you?"

The surprised man looked her over and said, "I would like to sweep you into my arms, rush you out of this store and up to my apartment, mix a pitcher of martinis, put on some soft music, then make passionate love to you, but what I really need is six pairs of hose!"

WARMED UP

The football team had done nothing but fumble all afternoon. So when a sub, warming up in front of the bench, dropped a ball that someone had flipped to him, a fan hollered, "Send him in, coach. He's ready!"

WASTEFUL

A salesman said to his wife one evening, "I'm glad I'm not in business for myself. I wasted the whole day."

WAVERING SURE SHOT

Two hunters huddled in their blind as a cold fog settled over the marsh. One took warming gulps from a jug of coffee, while his companion took nips from his fifth of bourbon. For hours, one gulped coffee, while the other downed whiskey.

Finally, a lone duck winged across the cloudy sky. The coffee drinker raised his shot-gun and fired. He missed. His now inebriated buddy, waved his gun unsteadily at the sky and fired. Down came the duck.

"I don't understand it," said the coffee drinker. "Here I've been drinking nothing but coffee for hours; I shoot and miss. You've been slugging down booze all the time; you shot and get a duck. How come?"

"Oh, thash nothin," said the staggering hunter. "When a flock that big comes along, I can't miss gettin one."

WAYWARD WOMEN

Two well-dressed matronly women entered the business office and approached an executive.

"Sir, we are soliciting funds for the welfare and rehabilitation of wayward women. Would you care to contribute?"

The executive answered, "Sorry, but I contribute directly!"

WEDDING ANNIVERSARY

A timid little employee approached his boss. "May I please, sir," he asked, "take next Wednesday off? My wife and I are celebrating our silver wedding anniversary."

The boss frowned, "Look here," he cracked, "do I have to put up with this every 25 years?"

WEEK-END WORRIER

My stocks are doing so badly, I even worry on week-ends!

WET THE APPETITE

Salesman: "But after getting my prospect up to the edge of the water, I couldn't make 'em drink."

Sales manager: "Who in heck ever told you that it was your job to make 'em drink? All you have to do is make 'em thirsty."

WHAT AND WHERE

An executive used to phone his wife from the office and tell her what he wanted to eat. Now, she calls him and tells him where.

WHAT BRAND?

Most Texans are pretty well inured in hard liquor. A visiting tourist was bragging in Fort Worth about being an expert.

"I can taste anything," he said, "and tell you right away what it is."

His Texan companion poured out a glass of stuff and handed it to the tourist.

The braggart took one gulp and gasped. "That's gasoline!" he cried.

"I know," the Texan said, "But it is it regular or high test?"

WHAT PILL?

The young salesman complained about his wife's constant reference to the pill. He's not sure if she means birth control pill or himself.

WHICH BROKER?

In the presence of a client he wished to impress, an executive flipped on his intercom switch and shouted to his secretary, "Miss Jones, get my broker."

"Yes sir," replied the secretary, "which one, stock or pawn?"

WHISTLING PROBLEM

One secretary can't decide about wearing glasses. When she wears them, the boys don't whistle. When she doesn't wear them, she can't see who whistled!

WHISTLING SOUND

The talk around the table at a sales executives' luncheon club turned to the question, "What's the most frightening sound you know?"

"A groan in the dark," said one man, "when you know nobody's there."

"I'd say the sudden buzz of a rattlesnake at your feet out in the woods when you don't have any boots on," said another man.

Finally, an older member of the party grunted, "I know a sound worse than all yours put together," he drawled. "A long, low whistle coming from an auto mechanic underneath your car!"

WHITE-WASHED CHIPS

One day the stock market dropped so fast that three blue chips turned white!

WIDE AWAKE CAR SALESMAN

The automobile salesman was really pouring it on about the better points of a used car. He said to the prospect, "For instance, the rattle in this car is a safety feature. It's so noisy, you can't fall asleep while driving."

WIFE MOTIVATOR

Sales manager: "Why do you call your wife 'my first wife'? You're still married to her. You've never had a second."

Salesman: "Of course, but you'd be surprised how that keeps her on her toes."

WIFE'S EMPATHY

The executive's wife, after a week-end trip said, "I had such a wonderful time with my husband. He thought I was his secretary!"

WIFE'S SELECTION

The sales executive was interviewing applicants to replace the secretary who was resigning. He asked the office manager to help him in making a selection.

The first candidate was a gorgeous, intelligent redhead.

The second gal was a sexy black-haired beauty, more intelligent than the redhead.

The third gal was an ugly 300-pounder—period.

After giving all three gals a test to determine their secretarial skills, he told his office manager that he was hiring number three.

The office manager commented, "I'm surprised. Why number three?"

The sales executive replied, "She's my wife's sister."

WINDOW DISPLAY

Shopper: "Can I try on the dress in the window?"
Store manager: "Why not, it might help business!"

WINNER PREFERRED

When the waiter served the tough-minded sales manager a lobster with a broken claw, he apologized and explained that the lobster had been in a fight with another lobster.

To this the sales manager roared, "Take this one back and bring me the winner."

WITCHCRAFT

The young executive had taken over $100,000 from his company's safe and had lost it playing the stock market. He was certain to be discovered. In addition, his beautiful wife had left him. Down to the river he went, and was just clambering over the bridge railing when a gnarled hand fell upon his arm. He turned and saw an ancient crone with a wrinkled face and stringy gray hair, dressed in a black cloak.

"Don't jump," she rasped. "I'm a witch, and I'll grant you three wishes for a slight consideration."

"I'm beyond help," he replied, and told her his troubles.

"Nothing to it," she said, cackling. "Alakazam! The money is back in the company vault. Alakazam! Your wife is home waiting for you with love in her heart. Alakazam! You now have a personal bank account of $200,000!"

The man, stunned to speechlessness, was finally able to ask, "What . . . what is the consideration I owe you?"

"You must spend the night making love to me," she smiled toothlessly.

The thought of making love to the old crone repulsed him, but it was certainly worth it, he thought. Together they retired to a nearby motel.

In the morning, the distasteful ordeal over, he was dressing to go home, when the old bat in the bed asked, "Say, sonny, how old are you?"

"I'm forty-two years old," he said. "Why?"

"Ain't you a little old to believe in witches?"

WITCH WIVES

Two salesmen were talking at the bar. One asked, "Have you seen that T.V. show, where the fella is married to a witch?"

Replied the other salesman, "Who isn't?"

WITHOUT ANY BREAKS

A credit bureau, trying to locate a man named Sexower, called the firm where he was supposed to work.

They asked the telephone operator, "Do you have a Sexower down there?"

"Oh my, no. We don't even get a coffee break."

WOMEN'S LIBERATION

The trouble with women in the business world is: If you treat them like men, they get mad. And if you treat them like women, your wife gets mad!

WONDERFUL CONTACTS

Two salesmen were talking, over a couple of short beers, and one said, "I made some wonderful contacts today!"

The other inept salesman said, "I didn't sell anything either!"

WORKING EVIDENCE

Finally, after an hour and a half the prospect came out of his office and said to the salesman waiting for him in the lobby, "I thought my secretary told you that I was out! What made you think I wasn't?"

Replied the salesman, "Your secretary didn't stop working all the time I was waiting."

WORKMEN'S COMPENSATION

Salesman to wife: "I didn't get the raise, but the sales manager broke my arm for asking, so at least I'll get workmen's compensation!"

WORTHLESS SALESMAN

Sales manager to salesman applying for job: "We will pay you all you are worth, after we try you out for a month."

Salesman: "I will not accept it, because I'm getting more than that with my present job.

WRONG ADVICE

A mousey little bookkeeper was terribly frightened by his boss. One day he told a fellow worker that he was sick, and his friend suggested that he go home.

"Oh, I couldn't do that," he said, "the boss would fire me."

"Don't be silly," said his friend, "he'll never know. He's not even in today."

Convinced that there would be no trouble, the little bookkeeper went home. When he got to his house, he looked in the window and saw his boss kissing his wife. He raced back to the office, and rushed up to his friend.

"A fine friend you are!" he shouted. "I nearly got caught!"

WRONG CALLS

Recently a man who bought a second-hand Edsel, which had a phone in it, complained to the dealer that sold it to him, "All the calls I get are from Desotos!"

WRONG CONTACTS

The sales manager of a direct selling company was asked to give his secret for always being able to get salesmen who were immediately successful for him.

He told his fellow sales executive, "I check on the applicant's appearance very closely. If I find that his pants show more wear than his shoes I don't hire him, because it shows he's making too many contacts in the wrong places."

WRONG DISCOVERY

Sales manager to inept salesman: "We have finally discovered what's wrong with our sales staff, it's you!"

WRONG FRIEND

One of life's disappointments is discovering that the friendly man who writes the bank ads isn't the one who makes the loans.

WRONG REHEARSAL HALL

A saleswoman entered a room in which the convention's next speaker, waiting to go on the platform, was pacing up and down, rehearsing his ad-libs.

Sales gal: "I recognize you. You're our next speaker. Tell me, do you ever get nervous before you speak?"

Speaker: "Get nervous? No, never!"

Sales gal: "Then what are you doing in the ladies room?"

WRONG SIZE

A dying wife motioned her husband to her bedside. "Jim," she said, "after I'm gone I want you to go on living. Find someone else. Give her my jewelry. Give her my home. Give her my Paris dresses."

Said the tearful husband, "I can't darling, I simply can't."

"But you must," the wife persisted. "You must."

The husband paused for a moment. "No, my dear," he said. "I really can't. You're a size 16 and she wears a size 10."

WRONG TELLER

"I went up to a bank window yesterday to make a deposit and the teller said, 'Sorry, that's another window. This one's for hold-ups!"

Y

YANKEE MERCHANDISING STRATEGY

A sophisticated woman visiting in New Hampshire was in a typical Yankee general store. One article on display particularly appealed to her, so she asked the proprietor the price of it.

Yankee storekeeper: "Ain't for sale."

City customer: "Why not?"

Yankee storekeeper: "It's the last one I have and if I sell it, how will anybody know what I'm selling?"

YES OR NO

The sales manager of a large firm was always trying to get his salesmen to think for themselves. One day, he received a telegram from one of his men who was enroute to Salt Lake City. It read: "Have lost my order pads. Shall I proceed to destination or return to the office?"

The sales manager wired back: "Yes."

Within an hour, another message arrived from the bewildered salesman: "Do you mean yes, I should proceed to destination or yes, I should return to the office?"

Whereupon the sales manager sent this laconic telegram: "No."

"YES SIR!"

Manager to assistant: "I don't like yes men. I want you to tell me what you really think even if it costs you your job."

YOU CAN'T TAKE IT WITH YOU

All of us have never had it so good, or parted with it so fast. We no longer have the concern of taking it with us, but making it last until we go.

YOUNG MAN'S EDUCATION

The self-made storekeeper had little patience with formal education. When a young man applied for work in his store, the owner said, "Sure I'll give you a job. Sweep up the store."

"But I'm a college graduate," protested the young man.

"Okay," said the owner, "I'll show you how!"

YOUNGSTER'S PLEDGE

Even kids know about income taxes. Last month a little five-year old saluted the flag and said, "I pledge my allowance to the flag."

"YOUR TURN!"

A salesman was driving an auto with his wife in the back seat and stalled his car on the railroad track with the train coming.

His wife screamed, "Go on! Go on!"

The salesman replied, "You have been driving from the back seat all day. I've got my end across. See what you can do with your end!"

YOU'RE ON CAMERA

A bank robber shoved a note across to the teller: "Put the money in a bag, sucker, and don't make a move."

The teller pushed back another note: "Straighten your tie, stupid, they're taking your picture!"

YOUTH'S POLITICAL STRATEGY

Republican boys date Democratic girls to have some fun before marrying Republican girls.

Z

ZEROED FINISH

Wife: "What did you tell the salesmen in your talk to them this morning?"

Sales executive: "Nothing!"

Wife: "Gosh, how did you know when your talk was finished?"

ZERO FUNCTIONS

A New York company decided to hire an efficiency expert to solve some of the problems of it's headquarters office staff, particularly the time spent by "pool" girls in the execution of their duties.

When the executive who had decided on the employment of the efficiency expert dictated his letter of acceptance of his services, his secretary set the office grapevine to work.

The gals congregated at the water cooler and at "other convenient conversational spots," and agreed that when asked questions about their functions within the organization, they would answer that their duties could be summed up in one word: "Nothing."

After interviewing three of the girls, the efficiency expert told the corporate executive, "Already I've discovered a problem—duplication!"

ZERO SALES RESULTS

The retail suit salesman was telling his wife how lousy sales had been so far this week.

Salesman: "Take Monday, I sold only one suit. On Tuesday, I didn't sell a single thing all day. And Wednesday was worse than Tuesday!"

Wife: "Why? On Tuesday you didn't sell one suit."

Salesman: "On Wednesday, the customer who bought the suit on Monday returned it and demanded his money back."

Part II

ONE-LINERS

FOR SALESMEN

AIR TRAVEL

- Airline executives are really humble these days—too many stack-ups and stick-ups to be stuck-up.

- You can breakfast in New York then take a jet to Los Angeles and upon arrival find out that your baggage is in Cleveland.

- One airline is so cheap that instead of showing movies the pilot buzzes drive-in-theaters.

- One flight was stacked so long over the airport that when the plane finally landed it was obsolete.

- The reason the airline gave for one of their flights being thirty minutes late was, "Tired gasoline."

AUTOMOBILES

- Thanks to air conditioning, couples in the back seat of the new model cars have a new worry—pneumonia!

- This car is so old that the clock on the dashboard is a sun dial

- One of the new cars at the Texas auto show is so big and plush, it has a walk-in glove compartment!

- Salesmen, if your wife wants to drive don't stand in her way!

- The best way to stop the noise in your car is to let her drive!

- You can usually tell when a woman is finished parking a car. She gets out of it.

- There's no reason why you shouldn't have a sports car, after all, you have the closet space for it!

- This auto is a Mother-In-Law model—it has a crank in the back.

- Times have changed, you call up a car dealer today and ask for a demonstration and he will send over three pickets!

- If you must drive while drinking be sure the radio in your car is turned up loud. That way you won't hear the crash.

- If it weren't for bumper stickers, some people wouldn't have any opinions at all!

- The buyer who looks under the hood of a used car doesn't know any more about it than the guy who used to look in a horse's mouth.

- The salesman's car was in such bad shape that when the monthly payment came due, he had to hire a cab to get to the finance company's office.

- My wife has been driving for two months and she isn't kidding when she comes home and says, "Guess who I ran into today?"

- General Motors auto workers got such a big increase, they can now finally afford a Lincoln.

- Did you hear about the auto worker who was offered a job as bank president, but he couldn't take the cut in salary?

- Where else but in America can you buy a '72 car while you're still paying off a '61?

- One of the big auto makers has a problem. They recalled faulty cars and got back 5,000 more cars than they built.

- The salesman's wife finally convinced him that they needed a new car—she wrecked the old one.

BASEBALL

- One of the good things about little league baseball is that it keeps parents off the streets.

- It was always my ambition to be a major leaguer, but who can shave that fast!

- Can you imagine unionized baseball? Three strikes and you're out. One strike and everybody is out!

- Once, when a baseball team was doing poorly at the gate, they got new players. Now they get a new city.

- To a New York Met fan the last two words of the "Star Spangled Banner" are *"Play Ball!"*

BUSINESS

- The president told the members of the board: "It's just a suggestion, but don't forget who is making it!"
- He who hesitates buys the stock two points higher!
- They say that the little man is back in the stock market. Does that mean that midgets are buying?
- Most brokers have only one problem these days—how to look sad with a smile on their faces.
- How can we balance the federal budget when we work only five days a week and the government spends seven days a week?
- A department store displayed a bikini that was so small that the price tag was bigger!
- Some people celebrate making the third payment of anything.
- Money isn't everything, but it comes in handy when you've lost your credit card.
- A bank robber called the F.B.I. and asked, "Mr. F.B.I., when will my pictures be ready?"
- Two men robbed a bank yesterday, but luckily the police got a description of the get-away car. It was either a 1965-66-67-68-69 or '70 Volkswagen!
- The line "Convenient to the bus lines," in real estate ads, simply means "No garage."
- They're having a tour of historic homes on the island next week. In some developments, any house that's still standing after seven years is historic!
- Did you know about the store that used to sell lettered sweatshirts, reading, "Money isn't everything," is now out of business?
- A woolen manufacturing company has announced the development of a moth that will eat synthetics.
- One office manager encourages all of his girls to make suggestions. Then after reading all their ludicrous ideas, he does things his way!

DIETING

- According to the life insurance table of weights and appropriate heights, the salesman wasn't fat—just five feet too short!

- Going on a diet is a matter of making up your mind that you'd rather look like you used to, than eat like you used to.

- The salesman bemoaned the loss of 122 pounds. She went back to her husband.

- Last Memorial Day, a paunch salesman tried on his World War II uniform and the only thing that fit was the tie!

- The prospect was so overweight that the insurance salesman tried to sell him a group policy.

- If you definitely want to do something about your weight, eat and increase it!

- The traveling salesman went on a 7-day diet last month and lost a week.

- A salesman's wife lost 12 pounds on a shopping trip—her charge plates!

- The best way to get your wife to go on a diet is to get her a mink coat three sizes too small!

DRINKING

- Some traveling salesmen should know their onions. They spend enough time picking them out of Gibsons!

- Every time a bartender makes a mistake a new drink is born.

- Most problem drinkers have a case history—Scotch or rye!

- Some men stop drinking as soon as they start buying.

- Whiskey may not cure a cold, but no remedy fails with such satisfaction!

- The saddest four words you finally hear at your favorite bar are "The bar is closed!"

- The salesman was an athlete! He suffered a football injury—fell off a bar stool, watching the Army-Navy game.

- The cocktail party was so dull that the salesman left with his own wife.

- After a few drinks some executives find that they speak quite fluidly!

• Once I gave up women and booze and it was the most boring twenty minutes of my life!

FOOTBALL

• You heard of the rambling wreck from Georgia Tech? Meet the boss, he's a total loss from Holy Cross.

• Nowadays the one who has the most difficulty staying in college is a losing football coach.

• The blonde senior wouldn't go out with the fullback because she was faithful to the end!

• A harried coach says his biggest problems are defensive linemen and offensive alumni.

• A midwestern university has ruled that no athelete be awarded a letter unless he can tell at a glance which letter it is!

GOLF

• If you watch a game, it's fun. If you participate, it's recreation. If you work at it, it's golf!

• The salesman arrested for hitting his wife with a golf club was only trying to *putt* her in her place.

• Some of the world's best golf scores aren't made with putters. They are made with lead pencils.

• Some golfers use carts instead of caddies because carts can't count!

• The salesman shoots golf in the low 70's. If it gets any colder he quits.

• There are a number of golfers who play a fair game, that is if you watch them closely!

• Americans are the most devout people in the world—if you consider golf a religion.

• The salesman's golf game is improving today. He just missed a hole-in-one by four strokes.

• It's not that the executive really cheats at golf. He plays for his health and a low score makes him feel better!

• A fair golfer is one who always quits after 18 holes or 90 strokes, whichever comes first.

INCOME TAX

- The night club owner made a joint return and the I.R.S. wound up with the whole joint.

- The only togetherness many couples have is when they file joint tax returns.

- This year's tax forms were unfair. For instance, you could list your wife as a dependent but not your mistress and they're much more expensive.

- There's a sense of pride in paying taxes in the U.S. The only thing is we could be just as proud for half the money.

- Did you ever notice that the guy who's going to save you a fortune by preparing your tax returns always lives in a one-room closet?

- We all have complete control over how we pay our taxes—by cash, check, or money order.

- Here's a way to get out of paying taxes for at least ten years. Don't pay them and you'll get ten years!

- If you read the income tax instructions very carefully, you quickly realize there are only two ways to fill out the form, and they're both wrong.

- Which has made the biggest liars out of Americans—golf scores or income tax returns?

- After sending in the income tax the farmer said, "Now I know how the cow feels about the milking machine!"

KIDS

- A kid who takes two hours to eat his lunch will grow up to become an executive.

- You don't walk into a kid's room these days. You have to knock. They've got rights!

- If you want your children to look up to you, simply walk into their room and turn off the television.

- One of the new generation of youngsters told his father, "Dad, I'm running away from home, call me a taxi."

- One of the greatest mysteries of life is how the boy you thought wasn't good enough to marry your daughter can be the father of the smartest grandchild in the world.

- If 18 year-olds are old enough to vote, they're old enough to drink! Politics will drive them to drink, anyway!

- The most important thing a salesman can do for his children is love their mother.

- A rich executive's son has been dating one of the family's servants, and they are very displeased. It's the butler.

- The most difficult job teen-agers have today is learning good manners without seeing any!

MARRIAGE

- Some wives are up until all hours removing spots from their husband's pants—five spots and ten spots!

- The salesman's son said he had been looking for a girl who could cook like his mother. Instead he found one who could drink like his father.

- Between their wives and daughters, some salesmen can't get on the phone, get in the bathroom and get out of the house.

- Home cooked dinners make a happy marriage. Unfortunately, most salesmen come home from selling too tired to cook dinner.

- About all that some wives know about good cooking is which restaurants serve it!

- Salesmen, the best way to put the boss in a good humor is to do the dishes for her.

- A salesman seldom tells his wife his selling problems until she wants to buy something expensive.

- When a wife doesn't mind her husband spending the night with the boys it probably means she's married to a scoutmaster.

- A talkative salesman is still unable to get in the last word when he argues with his wife—he can't stay up that late.

- A salesman and his wife, after twenty-five years of marriage, are planning their second honeymoon. She's going in June. He's going in August.

- It has been said that women are always ready to forgive and forget. I think it should be added that they never forget what they forgive!

- What some women are looking for is a man with a strong will—made out to them!

- Never trust your wife's judgment. Look at who she married!

- Second wives work out better than first wives. Like Avis, when you're No. 2, you try harder!

- The salesman's wife never knew where her husband was after midnight; more often, neither did he.

- Some salesmen's wives use the oldest birth control device in the world. They pretend they're asleep.

- The salesman discovered the mistake he made in his marriage—it was getting married.

- Behind many a successful man in this world, there's a woman, and behind her, his wife. And both of them telling him they have nothing to wear!

- The salesman and his wife have an understanding during the warm weather. If he comes home hot and too tired to eat, he doesn't have to cook.

- Most department stores are willing to give a woman credit for what her husband earns.

- A man will buy football tickets months in advance, but he'll wait until the day before his wife's birthday to order her gift.

- To err is human, to forgive is divine, and to get your wife to forget about it is terribly expensive!

- He is a well informed salesman. His wife has just told him what she thought of him.

- The salesman was complaining that his wife wanted only two things. First, to be sexy for him, and second, not to go near him.

- It was a double ring marriage ceremony. One around the bride's finger and one through the salesman's nose.

- Be as polite to your wife as you are to any other stranger.

- They now have drive-in theaters for married couples only. There's no kissing in the back seat, just arguing.

- Did you read about that husband who shot a lifeguard for giving his wife mouth-to-mouth resuscitation—six months after he saved her?

- What do you give a wife who has everything and none of it paid for?

POLITICS

- Nowadays it takes more money for a candidate to get elected than he's able to spend, once he gets in!

- Politics is the only profession in which a man can make a living solely by bragging!

- If some politicans said what they thought, they'd be speechless!

- Anybody who thinks there has never been a perfect man just hasn't been listening to campaign speeches!

- I'm going to vote a straight ticket this year, if I can find a candidate that's straight.

- Politicians make strange bed fellows, but they soon get accustomed to the same bunk!

- The politician interviewed was really quite persuasive in demonstrating how to be evasive!

- Political speeches on television make the commercials seem honest!

- A politican has to able to see both sides of a question, so he can go around it!

- You can take a politician at his word. The question is, what word?

- Defeated politician: "I'm glad I lost. Now I don't have to break all of my campaign promises!"

- You know, if we could use the money they spend in election campaigns, we could cure all the ills the politicians are complaining about!

- When a politican says he's going to stand on his record, that's only to keep you from checking on it.

- Actually, I've lost faith in politicians. I'm going to start voting for the ones who promise not to do anything!

SALES EXECUTIVE

- Behind every executive who has reached the top of the ladder is a wife telling him where to hang the picture.

- The sales manager has discontinued making long talks because of his throat—several salesmen have threatened to cut it.

- A man's true value is determined by how much his boss has to spend on a computer that replaces him.

- The businessman who says he is going to cut down his sales staff to save money, might as well stop his watch to save time.

- An executive met an old girl friend after many years and was upset because she had aged so much that she didn't recognize him!

- Effective sales management consists in showing average salesmen to sell like successful salesmen.

- A sales executive was overheard to state, "I'm working on my second million dollars. I gave up on the first."

- Executive, a clean desk could be a sign of overstuffed drawers.

- At some sales executive's club luncheons, members are all ears—for each other.

- If executive's wives only knew what their husband's secretaries thought of their bosses, they wouldn't worry.

- An executive discussing marriage claimed his wife made him a millionaire. Before she did this, he was a multi-millionaire!

- Let's always keep in mind that the sales department is not the whole company but the whole company is the sales department.

- Some executives have an answer to everything; a solution to nothing.

- The smart executive thinks twice before saying nothing.

- Be tolerant with a person who disagrees with you. After all, he has a right to his ridiculous opinions.

- Don't forget Mr. Sales Executive, ideas are great arrows, but there has to be a bow.

- Hard work never killed sales people, they say. However, it has scared some sales people half to death.

- 81.5 million people are working, no, change that, 81.5 million people have jobs.

SALES SPEAKERS

- Mr. Speaker, when your throat demands water, don't reach for a glass, instead reach for your chair.

- Many speakers stay awake at night preparing speeches to put others to sleep the next day.

- When he had finished his speech and left the head table, they called and called for him to come back. They finally *dared* him to come back!

- The speech started at 8:10 sharp and ended at 10:10 dull.

- The other night I fell asleep during a dull speech. The worst part of it was, that I was making the speech!

- Blessed is the speaker who has nothing to say and cannot be persuaded to say it!

- When your mind goes blank, turn off the sound!

- No one should speak, unless he's sure he can improve on the silence.

- One thing a speaker should remember: The mind can absorb only what the seat can endure.

- May your thoughts be worthy of your words and your words worthy of your thoughts.

- Speak when you are angry and you'll make the best speech you ever regretted.

- The sales manager is careful about his speech. The only time he has trouble with his English, is when he mixes it with Scotch.

- Be yourself as a speaker. But be yourself at your best.

- Mind your speech instead of speaking your mind!

- Professional speakers have the same problem as the world's oldest profession. It isn't the hours that ruin you, it's the amateur competition.

- The only gesture a speaker wants from his audience is applause.

- A good listener always allows people to hear their favorite speaker—themselves.

- Our guest speaker for tonight is really outstanding. He's been out standing by the door way.

- The world's best after-dinner speech is to hear, "Waiter, give me both checks!"
- The speaker who attended a convention of psychiatrists was asked to lie down and say a few words.
- The indestructibility of the public speaker is exceeded only by that of his listeners.
- He's such a talker, that he could talk a down-escalator into going up.
- They gave the out-of-town speaker the key to the city—to get out of town.
- If it weren't for speakers like me, you would never be able to determine how much better many other speakers are!
- Whenever you are on the platform, don't worry if anyone walks out in the middle of your speech. It's when they walk toward you that you'd better begin to worry!
- In some respects, making a speech is like a love affair. Any fool can start one, but to end it requires considerable skill.

SALESMEN

- Salesmen, eat, drink and make love today, because tomorrow your expense account may be cancelled.
- Enthusiasm puts more life into a salesman than booze and is easier to control.
- The salesman tried everything—flowers, candy, jewelry, furs— and they all worked.
- Confucius says: Salesman who covers chair instead of territory, always remains on bottom.
- A salesman who saved his money was once considered avaricious. Today the same salesman is considered a miracle worker.
- Salesmen, to climb the corporate ladder, if at first you don't succeed, try marrying the president's other daughter.
- Salesmen, always put off until tomorrow what you are going to louse up today.
- Some salesmen who claim to have twenty-two years of experience, actually have only one year of inept selling experience, multiplied twenty-two times.

- The inept salesman said, "I can't remember the name of the customer I'm trying to forget."

- Salesmen should always keep in mind that when you keep passing the buck, you won't make many bucks.

- The salesman was having trouble with his color television set every month. He couldn't make the payments.

- The successful salesman always keeps his hat on when in his office to remind him that he has no business being there.

- The salesman said, "I'm not an eighth-grade drop-out. I went the full eleven years!"

- The inept salesman is not looking for a customer he can trust, but for a customer who will trust him.

- Salesmen, do you want to know how to make a girl stop loving you? Marry her!

- Salesmen who frequent restaurants that feature topless waitresses are called "chestnuts."

SECRETARIES

- She's an amazing secretary. She's only been on the job two weeks and all ready she's a month behind in her work!

- She's sort of a slow typist, but she makes up for it in other ways. She can erase 40 words a minute!

- A certain secretary was so sexy that the birds and the bees studied her.

- Secretaries never seem to please anyone. If they're good, their bosses dislike them, and if they're bad, their bosses wives dislike them.

- The secretary couldn't sleep nights because she took too many coffee breaks during the day.

- The executive's secretary was so ugly that when he chased her around the desk, he walked!

- The modern fashionable dressed secretary wears pants to make her look like a boy and a flimsy blouse to prove she's not.

- When the struggling secretary stops struggling, she often discovers she doesn't have to be a secretary.

- I know a secretary who is so conceited, she has unlisted measurements!

- Executives do make passes at secretaries who wear glasses. Of course, it depends on their frames.

- Few things are more expensive than a secretary who is free for the evening!

SEX

- What is so attractive about the opposite sex is that it's so opposite.

- Did you hear about the girl who was arrested for being a dove in Times Square. The police found her in a doorway negotiating!

- If her lips are like fire and she shivers in your arms, give her up, she probably has malaria!

- Between mini-dresses and maxi-coats, a lot of us are looking high and low!

- When we asked a zoologist friend of ours, how porcupines have sex, we were told: "Carefully, very carefully."

Part III
DEFINITIONS
FOR SALESMEN

Account Executive: One whose padding is in his expense account, not his shoulders.

Attitude: A man's achievement in relation to his opportunity to achieve.

Bachelor: One who's footloose and fiancee-free.

Bachelor Salesman: A salesman who hasn't yet found a father-in-law he wants to sell for.

Banker: A financial executive who will gladly lend you money if you prove you don't need it.

Bankruptcy: A company's yearning exceeds it's earning capacity and it's creditors cash capacity.

Banquet: (1.) An affair where a speaker first eats food he doesn't want, and then proceeds to talk about something he doesn't understand to a lot of people who don't want to hear him. (2.) A plate of cold chicken and peas completely surrounded by warm appeals for contributions.

Bargain Sale: (1.) A device for transferring surplus goods from a basement to an attic. (2.) Anything women have enough money left to buy. (3.) Something a woman can't use at a price she can't resist.

Bore: Is a guy with a cocktail glass in one hand and your lapel in the other.

Born Executive: A fellow whose father owns the factory!

Born Loser: Is a guy who gets a blow-out in the spare tire in his car trunk!

Borrower: A man who tries to live within your means.

Budget: A method for going broke methodically.

Bulldozer: One who sleeps during after-dinner speeches.

Cadillac: What a doctor buys to not make house calls in.

Cocktails: Items in expense accounts which are responsible for staggering figures.

Coffee Break: The only 15 minute period in the morning when some office personnel stop doing nothing!

Committee: The unwilling appointing the unqualified to pool their ignorance to do the unnecessary.

Conference: (1.) A group of men who individually can do nothing, but who, as a group, can decide that nothing be done. (2.) The confusion of one man, multiplied by the number present! (3.) A meeting at which people talk about things they should be out doing instead of attending meetings.

Conservative: Anyone who takes his money out of the stock market to go to Las Vegas.

Consultant: (1.) A man smart enough to tell you how to run your business, but too smart to start one of his own. (2.) One who helps solve problems and then remains to become a part of the problem.

Credit: (1.) Instant debt! (2.) Everybody is buying on time, but nobody is paying on time.

D.B.L.I.T.Y.: Dress British, look Italian, think Yiddish.

Deceptive Packaging: Women with wigs, lipstick, eye shadow, false eyelashes and eye liner.

Devoted Husband: One who buys more expensive gifts for his wife than for his girl friend.

Devotion: Your wife allowing you to watch the Sunday football game on television.

Dieting: The art of keeping your mouth shut at the right time—such as breakfast, lunch and dinner.

Diplomat: A man who never tells a woman how nice she looks in a gown; he tells her how nice the gown looks on her.

Dishonest Politician: One who won't stay bought!

Drive-in-Bank: Where cars get a chance to see their real owner.

Economist: A man who would marry Raquel Welch for her money.

Ecstasy: Something that happens between the gin and tonic and the ham and eggs.

Education: The sum total of what you remember of what you originally learned.

Election Campaign: When the new candidates tell us how rotten the guys are that we elected last time!

Empathy: Putting yourself in the other fellow's shoes without putting yourself in his pants.

Emptiness: The dining room in a Poconos honeymoon lodge at breakfast time.

Executive Ability: Art of getting credit for all of the accomplishments of the people who work for you.

Executives Club Luncheon: A group of sales consultants completely surrounded by prospective clients.

Expense Accounts: Accounts deceivables.

Experience: It keeps a salesman who made the same mistake twice from admitting it the third time.

Expert: A fool a long way from home.

Face of Man: An autobiography.

Face of Woman: A work of fiction.

Fashion Expert: A gal who gets women to pay more money for fewer clothes.

Feminine Frustration: When a gal puts her bra on backwards and it fits!

Fictional Salesman: A man with the alcoholic capacity of the Hoover Dam, the witty tongue of Bob Hope, the stamina of a New York Jet linebacker, the sex habits of a rabbit, the ability to sell soap to the hippies, the diplomacy of a cheating husband, the persuasiveness of a job-hunting politician.

50-50 Marriage: Is when half the time your wife agrees with you and the other half of the time you have to convince her.

Financial Success: Spending what you have left after saving, instead of what is left after spending.

Flattery: The art of telling another person exactly what he thinks of himself.

Foolproof Diet: Eat only when the news is good.

Fraud: You lie to people to get their money.

Free Speeches: Are FREE because few are willing to pay for it.

Freedom of Speech: When the average husband talks back to his television set.

Frustration: (1.) When you're looking at *Playboy Magazine* and your wife is turning the pages. (2.) Shooting a double eagle and then finding out you played the wrong ball. (3.) A bald-headed Yippie.

Fuller Bust Man: Brassiere Salesman.

Go-Getter: His wife works and every afternoon he has to "go-get-her."

Go-Go Dancing: Calisthenics with a beat!

Golf: 18 holes, 17 of which are unnecessary and just put there to make the game harder.

Golf Cart: A conveyance used by the pro to transport the money he takes to the bank.

Good Clean Fun: A couple taking a shower together.

Green: A small patch of grass costing $2.00 per blade and located midway between a lake and an excavation full of sand.

Handicapped Golfer: One who is playing with the boss!

Hangover: The burden of too much proof!

Happily Married Couple: A husband out with another man's wife.

Head Start Program: A father who gets up early to beat his children to the bathroom.

Henpecked Husband: One who is afraid to tell his pregnant wife that he is sterile.

Holding Public Office: Like trying to dance in a nightclub, no matter what you do, you rub somebody the wrong way!

Honest Bartender: One who makes sure he makes less than the owner!

Honest Politician: One who will fulfill his campaign promises, no matter how dishonest he has to be to do it!

House Speaker: A husband who can master any tongue except his wife's!

Husbands Anonymous: An organization that, when a wife loads her husband with odd jobs around the house, a fellow "Husband Anonymous" comes over and talks him out of it.

Imagination: Like a girdle, it isn't how far you can stretch it that counts, it's the extent to which you can use it to shape up the subject matter.

Income Tax: The Washington version of instant poverty.

Income Tax Time: When millions of Americans tax their powers of deduction.

Incidental Job: One that doesn't pay enough to make it worth-while to invent a machine to do it.

Independent Salesman: He takes orders from no one!

Inept Salesman: An overrated stock clerk with an order pad and attache case.

Inexcusable Errors: Errors made by salesmen.

Justifiable Mistakes: Errors made by sales managers.

Inflation: After you get enough money to buy something, it isn't enough.

Informed Executive: A sales executive whose views are the same as yours.

Intellectual Secretary: One who can think up excuses that her executive boyfriend's wife will believe.

Interior Decorating: Spending what you haven't got on things you don't want to impress people you don't like.

Intoxication: When you feel sophisticated and can't pronounce it!

Introducer of Speaker: The guy who gets up to tell you that the best part of the dinner is over.

Intuition: The sense that enables a woman to contradict her husband before he says anything.

I.R.S. Cocktail: Two of them and you withhold nothing.

ISM: Internal Self Motivation.

K.I.S.S.: Keep It Simple Stupid.

Knowledge: Like money, the more you have of it, the less you need to brag about it.

Las Vegas: A place where the dice throw you.

Lawyer: A fellow who makes sure you'll get what's coming *to him!*

Lead Dependent Salesman: A dope addict who cannot move without a fix.

Legal Secretary: Any girl over eighteen.

Logic: An organized procedure of going wrong with confidence and certainty.

Loyal Bartender: One who never reveals a souse!

Luxury Article: A product that cost $10 to make, $20 to buy, and $30 to repair.

Marriage: (1) A business in which a man takes his boss along on his vacation. (2) A partnership brought on by yearning and then maintained by earning.

Marriage Anonymous: When a member feels like getting married, they send over a woman without make-up, her hair in curlers and barefoot.

Marriage Prosperity: That short period between the time you hide the money at home and the time your wife finds it.

Master of Ceremonies: The guy who tells you what's coming but not how to avoid it.

Metrecal Martini: You still see the same things, but the pink elephants are skinnier.

Mind: Like the stomach, it isn't how much you put in that counts, but how much it can digest.

Mini-Skirts: Never in the history of women's fashions has so little material been raised so high to reveal so much.

Mistress: A cutie on the Q.T.

Natural Born Leader: The son of the owner.

Neighbor: Someone who advises you on what to buy so he can borrow it later.

No: A word invented so that successful salesmen can manifest their professionalism!

Nominating Committee: A group with a long list of members they want to get even with.

Nudist Colony: A place where men and women meet to air their differences.

Old Age: When a man sees a pretty girl and it arouses his memory instead of his hopes.

Old-Fashioned Secretary: A gal who never drinks anything else.

One Year Guarantee: If you need service, you have one year to get it.

Optimism: A salesman's wife buying weight-reducing pills and a bikini.

Optimist: (1.) A man who is losing his hair and feels that he is gaining a forehead. (2.) A salesman who puts his shoes back on when the principal speaker says, "So in conclusion . . . ."

Orator: A speaker who is able to make loud noises from the throat sound like deep messages from the brain.

Panhandler: A proud man who would rather beg than accept charity.

Perfect Appliance: Something too heavy for the neighbor to borrow.

Persuasive Executive: One who can give a pretty secretary a letter to be re-typed a third time.

Persuasive Words: Truth told earnestly and eagerly.

Pessimist: A salesman who thinks that all women are bad. The optimistic salesman hopes so.

Philips Screwdriver: Vodka, orange juice and milk of magnesia.

Platonic Friendship: What develops when two people grow tired of making love to each other.

Politics: The art by which politicians obtain campaign contributions from the rich and votes from the poor, on the pretext of protecting each from the other.

Poverty: A state of mind induced by the neighbor's extended vacation in Europe.

Progress: When you replace a $90 a week clerk with a $200,000 computer.

Prospect: A man who would rather buy an automatic dishwasher than be one.

Prosperity: (1) The period between the last payment and the next payment. (2) Something businessmen create for politicians to take credit for.

Race Horse: An animal that can take several thousand people for a ride at the same time.

Race Track: A place where windows clean people.

Recession: A depression that got bogged down in prosperity.

Reputation: Character minus what you've been caught doing.

Russian Automobile: A car that only steers to the left.

Saint: A sinner who keeps on trying.

Sales Ability: What will get you to the top if the sales manager has no daughter.

Salesman: A guy who can convince his wife it's a shame to hide such a beautiful figure under a full length sable coat!

Salesman's Household: Consists of a salesman who works hard at selling and a wife who makes it necessary.

Salesmen's Aspirin: A customer who never says "No."

Salesmanship: The difference between rape and rapture.

Secretary: A girl to whom you pay a salary while she's killing time between high school and marriage.

Semi-Retired Executive: One who wears only the upper part of pajamas!

Sex: Fun without laughing.

Skilled Politician: One who can fling mud without getting dirty!

Slush Fund: Money set aside for snow removal.

Smog Cocktail: You have only one and you're polluted!

S. O. B.: Son of the boss.

Speaker: A man who eats a dinner he doesn't want, in order to get up and tell stories he doesn't remember, to listeners who have heard them already.

Speeches: (1) Like babies, they are easy to conceive but hard to deliver. (2) Like a bad tooth, the longer it takes to draw it out, the more it hurts.

Spoken Words: Thoughts of the brain, mood of the heart, tone of delivery!

Stimulating Speaker: A fellow who says things you would like to have thought of in the way you would like to have said them.

Suburban Husband: A gardener with sex privileges.

Success: When you have your name in everything but the telephone directory.

Successful Salesman: One who sells products that don't come back to customers who do.

Surplus: A shortage of shortages.

Tact: A matter of telling a man exactly what he thinks of himself.

Taxation: You pay income tax on what you put in your wallet and a sales tax on what you take out.

Taxi: A vehicle that is always never available when it rains.

Teenage Togetherness: Her hair curlers getting caught in *his* hair curlers.

Tee-Totaler: One who disputes your golf score.

"The Four Closures": A rock group made up of employees of a Baltimore bank.

Three-Way Communications: Tel-e-graph. Tel-e-phone. Tell-a-woman.

Through-Way: A parking lot with tolls!

Toastmaster: (1) A "Wisecrackonteur." (2) One who speaks with a few appropriated words.

Top Executive: One who can take as long as he wants to make a snap decision.

Top Money Earner: A man who earns so much that he has to borrow to pay his income taxes.

Trade Relations: Almost everybody would like to.

Traveling Salesman: A man who wishes he had as much fun on the road as his wife thinks he does.

True Alcoholic: A drinking man who goes into topless bars just to drink!

T.V. Sponsor: An advertiser who goes to the bathroom during the program.

Ultimate Husband: The husband who can make his wife feel sorry for the girl who lost her compact in his car!

Unemployed: A salesman, after the last sales call and until the next call!

Union Demand: To make more money and to make less products.

VHF: A T.V. set with Very High Financing.

Y.C.S.I.U.Y.T.I.: "You Can't Sell It Unless You Tell It."

YHTAPME: Empathy spelled backwards.

HANDBOOK OF SALES HUMOR FOR ALL SITUATIONS

by HENRI SAINT-LAURENT

Salesmen know that a laugh at the right time can soften up even the most stubborn prospects. Here is a book that provides literally hundreds of laughs for all such situations.

These crackerjack jokes and one-liners—all tried and tested over the past forty years—can help you "get your foot in the door" and make the sale.

You don't have to be a professional comedian to get laughs with these sure-fire stories. All you need is a sense of humor, the right joke, and you'll:

- **Break the ice**
- **Answer objections**
- **Get past the secretary**
- **Revitalize old accounts**
- **Win new customers**
- **Close faster**
- **Make better presentations**
- **Reduce cancellations**

Only the biggest "winners" are included here. Every punchline is designed for easy delivery and sure humor . . . and each story can be told in your own tone and style.

Moreover, these hilarious anecdotes are arranged by subjects for your easy reference. So whenever you anticipate a certain sales situation, simply turn to the corresponding section in the book and load up on sure laughs.

In no time you'll be able to use this effective means to making the Big Sales by . . .

- **Easing an uncomfortable selling atmosphere**
- **"Melting" the cold shoulder clients**

(continued on back flap)